THE PATTERN OF A DEPENDENT ECONOMY

THE PATTERN OF A DEPENDENT ECONOMY

THE NATIONAL INCOME OF BRITISH HONDURAS

BY

N. S. CAREY JONES

GREENWOOD PRESS, PUBLISHERS
WESTPORT, CONNECTICUT

The Library of Congress has catalogued this publication as follows:

Library of Congress Cataloging in Publication Data

Carey Jones, N S
The pattern of a dependent economy.

Reprint of the 1953 ed.
Bibliography: p.
1. National income--British Honduras. 2. British Honduras--Economic conditions. I. Title.
[HC142.Z9I52 1972] 339'.097282 77-157955
ISBN 0-8371-6178-9

Originally published in 1952
by Cambridge University Press

Reprinted by permission
of Cambridge University Press

First Greenwood Reprinting 1972

Library of Congress Catalogue Card Number 77-157955

ISBN 0-8371-6178-9

Printed in the United States of America

CONTENTS

PREFACE

The preparation of National Income tables for British Honduras for 1946 followed a conversation with the late Sir Gerald Hawkesworth, then Governor of the Colony, in 1947. Sir Gerald thought such tables would be useful, but we doubted if there was sufficient information available for them to be possible. They had to be based on data collected by others for different purposes, as I was fully occupied at the time and unable to undertake any special research to produce figures to fill any gaps which might appear when the data had been assembled. Sir Gerald gave me permission to use any unpublished information in the hands of Government of which I could get hold. During the following two years my ordinary work took me to nearly all the inhabited parts of the country and I was able, from conversations and discussions, unofficial and official, with many experienced men, to make valuable judgments, both for sorting out the figures which were accumulating and for making assumptions for filling in gaps in those figures. The tables had to be constructed in my spare time and were submitted to Government in almost their present form early in 1949. At this point it seemed that they might be of more than purely local and official interest and I sought permission of Government to publish them, together with such general descriptive matter as would make them intelligible to anyone not acquainted with the Colony. From this it was but a step to try to place the economy in a wider setting.

The present work has two aims: first, to show that a reasonably accurate national income study, in broad outline, can be made without overloading it with detail or spending an inordinate time in detailed research; and, secondly, to indicate some of the problems peculiar to a dependent economy by an examination in some detail of one. I hope I have been able to avoid the dangers of generalising from a particular, and often unusual, economy by comparisons with other colonies with whose economies I have been familiar, namely the Gold Coast and Northern Rhodesia, both countries as different from each other as they are from British Honduras.

In making the National Income tables I have based my work on that of Miss Phyllis Deane, with whom I had the benefit of discussions when she was preparing her calculations for Northern Rhodesia, and whose pioneer work, *The Measurement of Colonial National Incomes*, is the clearest exposition that I have seen of the methods and principles to be applied in such a study. There is an amount of information of a general kind on National Incomes, concerned mainly with principles and definitions, but which, based on well-documented societies, presupposes a quantity of statistical material available. The United Nations Statistical Office, however, in *National Income Statistics, 1938-1947*, reveals that for many of the thirty-nine countries and territories for which calculations have been made, nothing like the full information required for anything approaching an accurate study was available and that, even with the comparatively well-documented countries, often large assumptions had to be made and for various sectors of the economy rather generalised figures had to be put in. Miss Deane's work described clearly not only how she had constructed her tables but exactly where she had made assumptions and what their nature was. This detailed description of the application of the principles, describing the difficulties and how they were overcome, is invaluable.

I am convinced that the concept and use of national income studies should be familiar and intelligible to the interested layman as well as to the economist and statistician, if their full value is to be realised. As they are useful to governments in policy-making, so it is necessary that the public should understand, with its government, the reasons that have prompted a particular policy. To achieve this the rather arid desert of figures must be watered with general description showing the familiar background in a recognisable form and relating the figures to it. It is also important that where assumptions have been made they should be clearly stated, or one is liable to find oneself drawing from the tables as conclusions what are, in fact, none other than the assumptions which were made in building them up. Such conclusions may be perfectly correct, but they have only the accuracy of the original assumptions and are not valid deductions from the tables.

The assistance of those who deliberately helped me I have acknowledged in appropriate places. If the text, however, seems rather devoid of 'references' in support of statements made, this is because I owe a debt to the many persons whose brains, experience and knowledge I picked during three years, and cross-checked with that of others. British Honduras has been little written about authoritatively. The knowledge of the Colony is kept not in books altogether, but also in men's minds. While I can often remember who was the source of a piece of information, I cannot acknowledge it, as my informant would probably not recognise it placed in its wider setting and with my interpretation upon it. For much of what follows I can only state that such-and-such is what I know to be so.

Professor Frankel and Miss Deane have helped me constantly with sympathy and advice on points of principle. Mr A. F. A. Lamb, Conservator of Forests, Mr C. W. L. Fishlock, Director of Agriculture, and Mr R. K. Masson, Collector of Customs, have given me willing assistance with those parts of the economy with which they were most familiar. Needless to say, they bear no responsibility for any opinions expressed herein. My thanks are also due to Mr S. E. Tench and Mrs D. Gabourel, of the Audit Department, who never hesitated in the face of requests for reports and documents, typing and re-typing.

N. S. C. J.

NATIONAL INCOME OF

Income	$000	Output	$000
1. Profits from Estates	90	1. Agriculture	1,611
2. Profits from Trade, Business or Profession	1,590	2. Quarrying	3
3. Earnings of Farmers, Tradesmen and Small Shopkeepers working on own account	3,414	3. Fishing	110
4. Salary Earners	1,397	4. Forestry	2,300
5. Wage Earners	3,062	5. Manufacturing and Repair	990
6. Interest	97	6. Construction	586
7. Rents, Royalties, etc.	920	7. Transport and Communications	556
8. Remittances from Abroad	237	8. Commerce	1,653
		9. Recreational Service	46
		10. Professional Service	441
		11. Public Service	907
		12. Personal Service	302
		13. Other	307
		14. Housing	668
		15. Income from Abroad	327
	10,807		10,807

BRITISH HONDURAS, 1946

EXPENDITURE	$000	$000	$000
1. Consumption:			
Food, drink and tobacco	4,522		
Clothing	1,304		
2. Other Personal and Private Capital Expenditure	5,541		
		11,367	
3. Less Indirect Taxes		941	
		10,426	
4. Plus Subsidies		108	
		10,534	
5. Government Expenditure on Current Goods and Services		1,415	
6. Government Investment		545	
			12,494
7. Remittances Abroad			25
			12,519
Less Disinvestment:			
8. Net Government Receipts from Abroad		947	
9. Investment by Foreign Companies		827	
10. Income of Foreign Missions		150	
			1,924
			10,595
11. Saving			212
			10,807

BRITISH HONDURAS, 1946

Expenditure	%	%	%
1. Consumption:			
Food, drink and tobacco	42·04		
Clothing	12·12		
2. Other Personal and Private Capital Expenditure	51·51		
		105·67	
3. Less Indirect Taxes		8·75	
		96·92	
4. Plus Subsidies		1·00	
		97·92	
5. Government Expenditure on Current Goods and Services		13·15	
6. Government Investment		5·07	
			116·14
7. Remittances Abroad			0·24
			116·38
Less Disinvestment:			
8. Net Government Receipts from Abroad		9·27	
9. Investment by Foreign Companies		7·69	
10. Income of Foreign Missions		1·39	
			18·35
			98·03
11. Saving			1·97
			100·00

I. THE PURPOSE OF THE STUDY

Before undertaking a study of this kind some idea of the possible uses of the tables is necessary in order to decide what form they should take. The final form is determined by: (*a*) the information available, and (*b*) the possible use of the tables.

The former is an overriding determinant, but even so, with a certain amount of inference based on experience, a number of variations are possible. The latter is a more difficult point. One can set up one's tables with an eye either on other national income calculators or towards the people or government of the country with which one is dealing. Clearly, if the purpose is to contribute to world economic studies, it will be important to cast one's tables in a form which will be comparable with those of other areas. The United Nations Statistical Office has made recommendations for the uniformity of plan, for the inclusion and exclusion of certain items and for the use of similar definitions, which so far no single country has applied entirely. In fact, no two countries produce exactly the same national income statistics. In any event, limitations of data must often make the fulfilment of their ideals impossible. Quite apart from this, it is a question whether the international comparability of such statistics should override local needs. At the present stage of the study of national incomes, while it may be of interest to compare the measure of the economies of different areas, and of practical value where highly developed countries are concerned, where plans for the integration of economies are being made, where economic policy is directly connected with national income figures and where, as in the United Kingdom, the national income and the budget are closely allied, the same hardly applies to dependent and under-developed economies. Even the United Nations Statistical Office has not yet laid down rules for national income studies of dependent territories where subsistence agriculture and migrant labour play a large part in the economy. Of the many uses of national income studies given in *National Income Statistics, 1938-1947*, only one refers particularly to under-developed territories: 'The problems of the under-developed countries and proposals for raising their standards of living also require a detailed knowledge of the national income and its components.'

There is also the use which the distant planner or overseas investor might make of the study as a general economic picture. He could use it also to check more detailed information from other sources, possibly interested sources. What other use is likely to be made of a colonial income study? The answer is largely unknown because there have been so few of them, and then only for isolated years. The use will vary from colony to colony according to the degree of control exercised over the economy by the colonial government and the nature of the economic machinery. There is no doubt that, as elsewhere, in most colonies government is an increasingly important factor in the economy and its activities have a greater influence than ever before. Taxation has increased and government investment, especially under the Colonial Development and Welfare Acts, is often a major economic influence. During the war colonial economic and financial departments developed, and, with wartime control and the creation of supplies departments, not only did government knowledge of and interference in colonial economies grow but the departments themselves became more practised in the application of economics to policy. Of the past it would probably be true to say that the governments of officials in the colonies pursued policies which were the resultant of the various forces that played on them, of the various pressures to which they were subjected, such as large industrial interests, chambers of commerce, and the restraining hand of the Colonial Office. They were not themselves a force. Their effects on the economies of their particular colonies were large but unrelated. Any reasonably vocal sector of the economy could get the policy which it desired, provided that it did not conflict with other, equally vocal, sectors. Government policy was negative rather than positive, it reacted rather than planned, and was especially timid of interests which were vocal in the United Kingdom rather than locally.

Nowadays policy tends to be more positive. Development is 'planned', though planning takes place without that thorough economic knowledge on which it should be based. Colonial 'planning' is similar to what is an administrative or executive department of planning in more developed countries. It is not an integration and direction of the parts of the economy but a table of priorities for capital works. Nevertheless, colonial governments do take a lead now—instead of following—in close consultation with the representatives of the local community. In fact, together with a change to positive policy-making, there has been a decrease in the authority and power of Government. Most colonies now have an unofficial majority on their legislative council (or other representative and legislative body). The effect of this is that any particular point of policy, any specific application of it, can be prevented by the legislative council. Thus while governments increasingly have policies they are increasingly unable to ensure that they are carried out. This difficulty is being met by broadening the basis of representation, so that sectors which had no voice before now have one, and a purely sectional policy, devoted to only one interest, becomes more difficult; and by taking representatives into the Executive Council where policy is formulated, and making them share in policy-making and the responsibility for policy. (It is interesting to note that an eagerness on the part of representatives to take part in the formulation of government policy is matched often by a reluctance to bear any responsibility for it when formulated, if any of its aspects do not prove popular. This is probably a 'teething trouble' of the new system, as representatives are traditionally elected in opposition to government, which has in the past been reluctant to explain its policies, for, as we have seen, it rarely had any.)

The next stage seems to be the complete responsibility of the representatives for policy, with the officials acting only in an advisory and administrative capacity. It is in the transitional stage that national.income studies begin to have an especial value, although they will be even more valuable in the final stage if colonial politics are not to become a battleground of sectional interests with the carefully fostered civil service of (what may be termed) 'national' outlook wasted.

It is perhaps an exaggeration to say that colonial civil service governments have become more positive in themselves, although they have the appearance of being so. They now purport to do certain specific things for a colony, generally under the heading of 'development', whereas in the past the maintenance of law and order and peace for trading was the chief aim. A more accurate description of what has happened might be to say that the war, movements in Britain, and a rising tide of nationalism rooted in colour-consciousness, have combined to release new forces which are liable to disturb the basic government function of maintaining law and order. These new forces have therefore been made constitutionally vocal and have tended to upset the equilibrium of colonial politics. As a first step to counter this a pressure, taking the form of 'development and welfare', which it was hoped would equal the pressure of the new forces, was applied to the colonial governments by the Colonial Office. This gave the colonial governments an appearance of being positive. The structure was shored up, it was hoped for some time, while alterations to the building were made to render it more suitable to the changed conditions. In practice the Colonial Office pressure is not proving equal to the pressure of the new forces, and a new and revolutionary equilibrium is being achieved in the more advanced colonies, such as Jamaica, by the extinction of the system of government by officials. It must be a primary aim of the Colonial Office, though publicity and propaganda may direct attention elsewhere, to maintain equilibrium in the colonies. It is clearly responding fairly rapidly to disequilibria, but often its specific economic responses are faulty for lack of proper data. National income studies should help to overcome this and make it possible to anticipate disequilibria in the economic sphere and such in the political sphere as are dependent on economics.

It is easy to talk in general terms of 'new forces' and 'nationalism' without explaining what one means, thereby causing confusion where enough exists already. Nationalism, colour-consciousness, the interests of the working classes or the underdog, and democracy, are all generally confused in one glorious sentimental muddle. It is strange, for example, to see those who would improve the lot of the worker advocating the granting of self-government to colonies, thereby throwing away their ability to improve his lot and handing him over to a state where they cannot ensure his being safeguarded from exploitation. It suggests an over-anxious desire to use arguments of nationalism and self-determination in order to shift one's responsibilities on to other shoulders, before seeing that the owners of the other shoulders are prepared to bear the responsibility.

It is no part of my aim, however, to discuss politics, with which I am not acquainted. But there is one interesting point which is, perhaps, worth noting about nationalism and the counter to it. On the whole it would be true to say that the two main influences in the creation of nationalism are, first, the growing urban populations composed of different tribal or racial groups, often existing in squalid conditions and without the social satisfactions of tribal life, who must seek an outlet or a satisfaction from some other source; and, secondly, the growth of an educated black class which cannot easily be absorbed into the ruling class and which feels frustrated in its reasonable search for power and position. This class is able to exploit the dissatisfaction of the new townsman and rouse 'national' feeling on a colour basis. In West Africa today the nationalism of the tribe and the nationalism of the black townsman are still contending. The point I would make is that the 'new forces' arise as much from social and even spiritual as from economic disequilibria, but they are being combated (or their disruptive element is) by economic counter-forces only. The economic counter-forces are as liable to create disequilibria as to remove them. Too much absorption with trade returns or general accretions of wealth to the community are apt to mask social stress and distress in detail (until the disease erupts in social and political strife). Governments naturally want a yardstick to measure the success of their activities, but trade returns and economic statistics are altogether too simple. It is natural for governments to use them, partly on account of their simplicity, but also because they reveal where the sinews of government, taxation, may be strengthened. But government is not all economics, and healthy trade returns may well conceal a sick society. No economic policy should be without an accompanying social policy.[1]

Indeed, an economic policy should be pursued for its social effects, rather than regardless of them, with Government later trying to mop up the milk which its own economic policy has spilt. This is, of course, only another way of saying that man does not live by bread alone. The 'bread' is necessary to life, and, as we shall see later, the successful survival of British Honduras requires action in the economic field. What form that action takes should be determined not merely with a view to achieving the maximum bread but to achieving a happy and stable society as well. It is often said that the African was happier before he began to enjoy the benefits of white civilisation. It is obvious enough that poor societies are often happier than rich ones. Evans-Pritchard, in his studies of witchcraft in the Sudan, has done a lot to explode the 'darkest Africa' myth of the native living in constant terror of witchcraft and has shown that, in fact, witchcraft does resolve the intangible prob-

[1] Even national income figures may be used as a yardstick in a dangerous way. The Kenya Development Committee laid down as a basic principle governing development—'to use the natural resources of the country, including manpower, in a manner calculated to increase the National Income of Kenya in the shortest space of time so as to raise, as soon as possible, the standard of living of the majority of the inhabitants'. This implies that increasing the national income will result in raising the standard of living of the majority of the inhabitants. There is no logical necessity for this. The national income can be raised in such a way that the few will benefit at the expense of the many. Unless the clause following 'so as to raise' is considered to define the manner in which the national income should be increased, the aim of raising the standard of living of the majority will not necessarily be achieved. That depends on the arrangements for distributing the national income and can even be achieved without increasing it.

lems of life in an eminently practical way and is conducive to happiness.[1]

Partly, of course, a poor society tends to be happy because it is a small society, and every individual in it has a status and function, in part customary and accepted, and in part dependent on his own personality and its interplay with the other personalities of that society. In a large society the individual has no existence as an individual. He is lost in an amorphous mass of people. No one is interested in him and, if poverty is added to his lot, his state is much worse than before. This is the problem of the large colonial town, which offers a great field for constructive sociology.

The problem of making a large town a proper social organism has probably not been satisfactorily solved anywhere. The solution has not been attempted in most colonies. The late Godfrey Wilson, in his studies of the urban African in Northern Rhodesia, was a lonely pioneer in attempting to find out something about life in colonial towns, and that is far removed from constructing a social life in them, which should be the end. Sir George Beresford Stooke, when Chief Secretary of Northern Rhodesia, made an imaginative and constructive contribution to the problem with his policy for creating African suburbs which would have a unified structure and life of their own. Government policy is most firmly based when one can give a satisfactory answer to the question, 'What will happen to Smith, Brown, Kwamina, Ticky Tembo, Njeroge, as a result of it?' Even the provision of varying social interests, such as occupy Europeans, would probably go a long way to dissipate the dissatisfactions of the new townsman. For want of a social organisation in which he can take a respected and useful place and exercise his abilities, a man will tend to seek

[1] Science explains how one gets malaria, by being bitten by a malaria-carrying mosquito. But, what I want to know is why that particular mosquito which gave me malaria bit me, instead of biting my friend who was with me. This question, which science does not pretend to answer, witchcraft does. I have been bewitched and, apart from the satisfaction of knowing *why* (teleologically) I suffer, there are certain practical steps that I can take, such as going to a witch-doctor who will find the witch and take steps to remove the spell.

comfort in the emotional excitements of nationalism, race-hatred, etc.[1]

This is not to say that economic counter-forces are useless. They are not, but it is all the more important to apply them properly so that they do in fact remove disequilibria and not create them. It is sometimes assumed that development is good *per se*, as an end, that so much more exported, so much more produced, increases the sum total of a community's happiness. It is true to a large extent, but the object should be the creation of prosperous *societies* and not merely prosperous economic units. That is why in a later chapter I have discussed the development of British Honduras from the point of view of its present inhabitants, whom I have learnt to respect and to love, and whose way of life I have enjoyed sharing, rather than simply from the point of view of increasing the output from a given land area. The latter point of view was naturally dominant in the Report of the Evans Commission, which was only incidentally concerned with the local inhabitants.

There is often a great deal of unco-ordinated economic information on government files and records. (Some of this I was able to find; some came my way fortuitously in connection with other matters.) Indeed, for the student of a colonial economy there would be much value in Government publishing an annual statistical abstract containing the miscellaneous data that come its way, and which otherwise get buried and lost in files. This would be especially valuable in colonies which cannot afford their own statistical offices, as it would provide accessible material for the private investigator who would do the work at no expense to the colony. Much of this information naturally seeps into the minds of officials in the course of their work and in time their 'subconscious' will co-ordinate it in a highly subjective way. As a result government officials are better informed than the rest on the general economy, although

[1] Today a man rarely has the possibility of seeking outlets of power and position in unrestrained capitalism, and now that capitalism no longer has the philosophical backing of classical economics, when it was shown to be virtuous and in the general interest, many would not wish for that specific outlet.

even this knowledge may be gravely distorted, dependent as it is on the particular facts which happen to make it up. It never makes a coherent picture, as without certain logical tools of analysis the mind seems capable of entertaining mutually contradictory propositions even at the same time.

While policy was negative, and generally expected to be negative, this was not so significant. Now it is important (unless all talk of development and planning is propaganda) to bring the facts together and show the various pieces of information in their proper relation to one another. With the increasing participation of the representatives in government, it is more than ever desirable to publish the information, and national income studies are a handy way of making a mass of information and reasonable deductions available in assimilable form and in their correct proportions. Even if colonial governments do not really plan for many years to come, the sort of 'planning' which they do will be better if based on a sound appreciation of the pattern of the economy, and they will more easily convince the colony of the virtues of their plans. There are generally current in colonies what might be termed economic myths, often the result of propaganda. An interested group that makes a lot of noise is liable to be thought unduly important. That group may bring undue influence to bear on Government because of this impression and may persuade Government that its needs should override those of some other sector. A national income study suitably broken up makes this more difficult to achieve, more especially if the true position becomes common knowledge.

It is important that the information should be in an easily assimilable form. The Jamaica Statistical Office has recently produced an estimate of the national income of the island for 1943, with projections to 1946, which is beautifully documented and supported by a mass of detail. It must be the envy of every economist who lacks a statistical office behind him when making such an inquiry. It also pays tribute to the inspiration of Miss Deane, but where Miss Deane goes into a great deal of detail for methodological purposes, the Jamaica Statistical Office follows her without her reason. One cannot help feeling that this thick tome, with its mass of detail used for building up the tables, will appal alike the civil servant and the representative, busy as they are with committees and boards and their own work, and that it will never serve the purpose for which, presumably, it was intended. The trees, magnificent as they are, are too luxuriant and obscure the wood. In fact, in the present stage of colonial economics and politics it may be doubted whether such an approach is worth all the trouble. Professor Frankel has recently described such an approach as the application of the accounting system of General Motors to 'the operation of a wayside petrol station run by a man whose main livelihood is obtained with the assistance of his wife and children from an agricultural allotment'.[1] For present purposes in the colonies it would seem that a simpler approach which short-circuited a lot of the detail (certainly in presentation) would be sufficient. The picture would be less accurate, but not so much less; its outlines would be clearer; it would be cheaper and easier to produce.

There is, I think, a real difference between a colonial national income study and others. It might be better to use the term 'colonial income' for territorial units that are both economically and politically dependent, were it not that so many of the problems met in a colony are found in varying degrees in politically independent, but economically dependent, units. A 'dependent economy' is mainly one which is under-capitalised ('under-developed') and cannot raise the capital for its own needs within its own borders. Hence it depends on outside sources for its capital and development. This limits its activities to the extent that it has to provide attractions for foreign capital and maintain such conditions that it will be willingly and fearlessly invested there. In the main this study is concerned with the activity of foreign capital in a territory which cannot provide its own. A colony which is also a dependent polity is further limited. It can only plan in a very special sense. In some cases its economy may be directed, partly, with a view to

[1] Review of Miss Deane's *Measurement of Colonial National Incomes* in the *Economic Journal*.

furthering the economy of the 'mother' country. Direction on behalf of the mother country may be of equal benefit to both, but it may not. Apart from this a colony will tend to be bound by fairly rigid financial rules. The exercise of monetary control will almost certainly be limited. Investment is out of its hands and the checking or stimulating of investment by varying interest rates is beyond it. Its banking institutions will be responsible to headquarters elsewhere. (The recent establishment of a central bank in Ceylon was one of the first signs of an attempt to get full control of its own affairs by a newly emancipated colony.) [1]

Where the attractions for the owner of the foreign capital to settle are small, a colony is peculiarly liable to see the disappearance of the capitalist with his capital (whether in goods or money), leaving the country with hardly a trace. An example appears in the *Forest Department Report for 1948*. 'One of the large American firms working partly in this Colony and partly in Guatemala has removed entirely to Nicaragua owing to political difficulties in Guatemala.' With it went the whole of its capital equipment. There is always this likelihood that the

[1] 'The Currency Boards, whatever detailed problems they have in the detailed management of their funds . . . have no worries about whether they can or should maintain a given rate of exchange. Their ability to do so is guaranteed by the holding of reserves which in nearly all cases exceed the total face value of all the currency issued; and the question of whether the rate should be maintained is outside their scope. Equally, nobody in a colony has the responsibility of determining a credit policy for the colony. Individual banks may, of course, have their own credit policies, may be more or less venturesome, but so far as there is a general credit policy it is that of the United Kingdom. In such matters there is in effect no more room for a policy for an individual colony than there is for a policy for an English county. In each case the local demands for credit are met out of a larger (for practical purposes an infinitely larger) pool. Local variations in the need for currency or bank money are absorbed by the larger pool almost unnoticed. The amount of such local currency or bank money in use is determined by many influences—the desire of local inhabitants to hold cash, the activity of trade, the willingness of outsiders to remit new funds for local investment, etc.—but not by any conscious monetary decisions of the colonial authority. The specifically monetary influences to which the colonial economy is subject are solely those of United Kingdom policy' (*Monetary Systems of the Colonies*, published by the *Banker*). This admirable little booklet touches on some of the problems of monetary dependence.

foreign capital will simply give employment to labour for a period and then disappear, possibly after taking very large profits, leaving no permanent improvements, adding nothing to the wealth of a country in either physical or monetary terms, but rather reducing such natural wealth as existed before. Many fortunes must have been made in British Honduras, but the only trace that remains is enormous freehold estates whose forest has been cut out and whose agricultural potential has hardly been tapped.

Besides all these basic differences, there is a difference in the purpose of a national income study of a colonial territory not so much in the ways in which it can be used but in the ways in which it is likely to be used. It also produces problems of definition. Marshall, in his *Principles of Economics* (5th edition), says: 'The labour and capital of the country, acting on its natural resources, produces annually a certain net aggregate of commodities, material and immaterial, including services of all kinds. This is the true net national income or revenue of the country, or the national dividend.' Where the capital is not *of* the country, where saving is so small as to be a negligible factor in investment, definitions have to be amended. This is one reason for the definition adopted here, which is discussed in more detail in a later section.

I have, in the following notes and tables, tried to set out in summary the various factors in the economy of British Honduras broadly in their true proportions, and in a form which can be clearly grasped. The picture, as will be seen from the notes to the tables, is in part generalised. It relates to the year 1946, but in some instances figures for other years have been imported into the tables to fill gaps, where the changes have been thought not to be significant. It is thus a general picture of the economy in the immediate post-war period and a fairly prosperous time. In 1949 a severe drought and outside economic forces would have affected the figures but not the general picture. Certain changes are foreshadowed, the full effect of which will be felt in the present decade. Without knowing the policy which will be pursued, it is impossible to anticipate them by projecting the tables forward. The work falls short of some of the high aims of national income studies, but, in a first study of this particular economy, should be a reasonable start. The tables are accompanied by notes, partly describing the sources of information, the difficulties of assessment, the assumptions made and the definitions used, and partly by general descriptions of the economy intended to fill in the background to the figures and show what interrelations are apparent. The explanations are thus of two kinds : (*a*) for the economist-statistician, explaining the figures themselves, and (*b*) for the layman, describing the general picture.

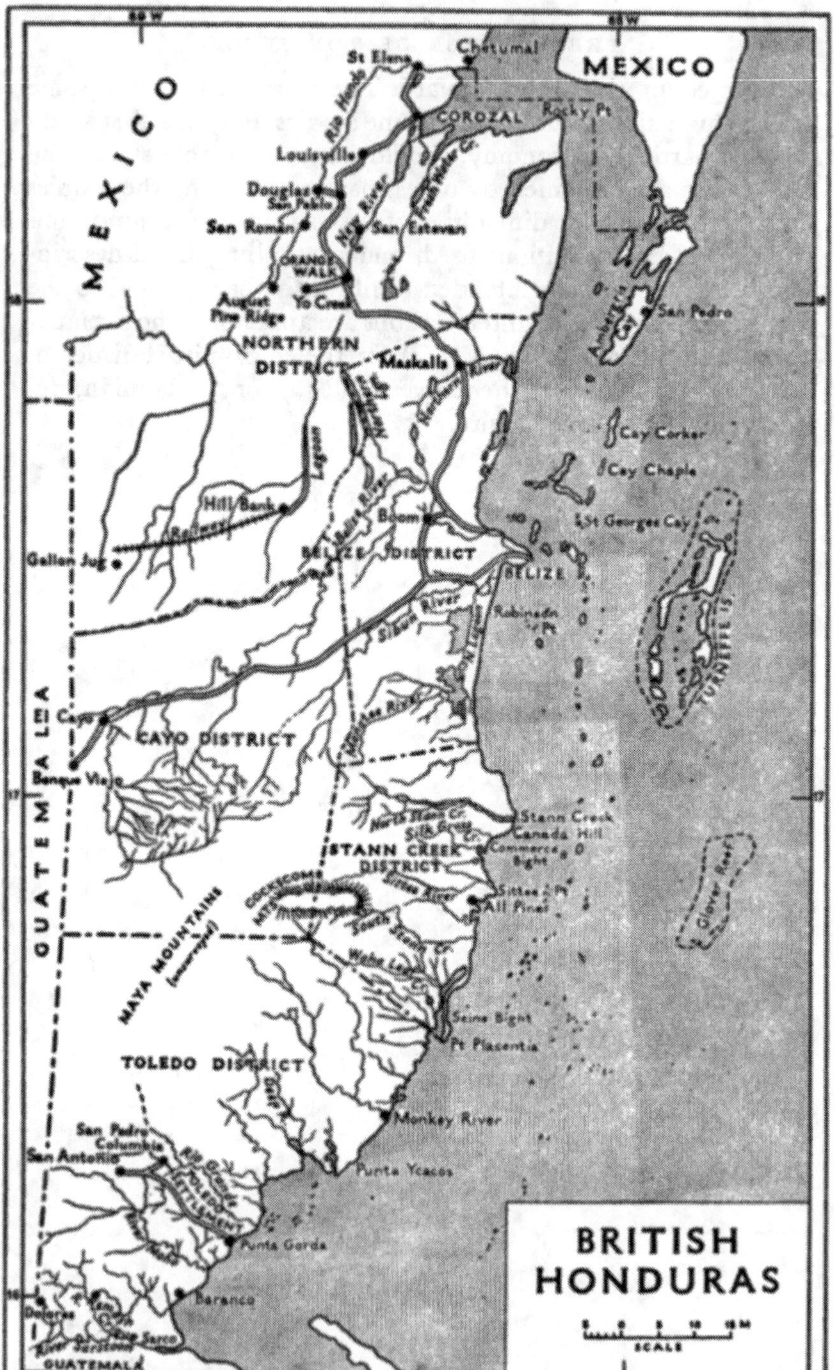
MEXICO
MEXICO
Chetumal
St Elena
COROZAL
Rocky Pt
Louisville
Douglas
San Pablo
San Roman
San Estevan
ORANGE WALK
August Pine Ridge
Yo Creek
San Pedro
Ambergris Cay
NORTHERN DISTRICT
Maskalls
Cay Corker
Cay Chaple
Hill Bank
Railway
Boom
St Georges Cay
Gallon Jug
BELIZE DISTRICT
BELIZE
Sibun River
TURNEFFE IS
Cayo
CAYO DISTRICT
Benque Viejo
GUATEMALA
Stann Creek
Canada Hill
Commerce Bight
STANN CREEK DISTRICT
All Pines
Glover Reef
COCKSCOMB
MAYA MOUNTAINS (unsurveyed)
Seine Bight
Pt Placentia
TOLEDO DISTRICT
Monkey River
San Pedro Columbia
San Antonio
Punta Ycacos
Punta Gorda
Barranco
Dolores
GUATEMALA
BRITISH HONDURAS
SCALE

II. GEOGRAPHICAL AND HISTORICAL BACKGROUND

A brief note is necessary to explain the general background to the figures and make clear some of the terms and places referred to later.

British Honduras is roughly a rectangle the size of Wales, on the eastern coast of Central America, bisected from west to east by the Belize River, which rises on the western frontier with Guatemala. The northern half is a flat plain with two large, deep rivers flowing to the north: the New River, and the Rio Hondo which forms the boundary with Mexico. Between the sea and the New River the land is low-lying, with lagoons, swamps, scrub-marsh, pine and other forest intermingled. Most of this land is probably unsuitable for agriculture, but it contains a few settlements. The climate gets drier to the north and the forest carries the best mahogany, but also the slowest growing. Between the New River and the Rio Hondo the ground is slightly higher and the soil, a limestone marl, is suitable for agriculture. This area carries the greatest density of villages. The southern half of the Colony is mountainous, broken country, covered with dense forest, the greater part being still unexplored. Even this forest, however, appears to be secondary growth, as frequent traces of early Mayan settlement are to be found, including pottery, mounds and contour-ridges, in places now covered with forest. Mahogany does not appear to be indigenous in the south, but its occurrence is connected with early Mayan clearings. The rainfall increases from north to south, from 40 ins. to 200 ins. per annum. The high rainfall in the south adds to the cost of agriculture, as the land has to be kept clear of a luxuriant natural growth. A barrier reef runs for the whole length of the coast at a distance of 7 to 25 miles and is dotted with small islands. Inside the reef the water is very shallow and only at Stann Creek can vessels of moderate draught approach the land. The reef-protected waters provide a safe sea for the small motor boats, sailing boats and dorys which ply up and down the coast.

Settlement has been almost entirely from the sea, penetrating along the rivers and lagoons, and on the coastal strip and the cays. It is still concentrated in these regions. The two northern rivers are navigable for a considerable distance and the Belize River, at one time by means of pitpans (shallow barges), then tunnel-screw motor boats, with occasional hauls over runs, as far as El Cayo on the western border (a journey of a week or ten days). The Mayan Indians have, however, settled in the interior. Road building is extremely expensive, owing to the marshy nature of the ground. The Belize–Corozal road, opened before the war, duplicates water transport for most of its route, and for the rest runs through mainly barren scrubland. The Belize–El Cayo road, opened in 1947, taps a fertile region on the western frontier, and settlement is now taking place along most of its route. The Stann Creek valley road taps a rich citrus and (erstwhile) banana area. The Punta Gorda–San Antonio road connects the East Indian successors of the American settlers and the biggest Mayan centre with the sea. All other communications are by horse and mule along forest trails.

The earliest recorded settlement occurred about 1638 and a flourishing trade in logwood grew up; prices in the 17th century were about £100 a ton, compared with £6 a ton just before the trade disappeared. The settlement at Belize and St George's Cay numbered 700 whites in 1670, more British people than are there today. It seems that Belize was the chief of many settlements along the Central American coast from Yucatan to the Mosquito Coast of Nicaragua (they have left English-speaking populations in the Bay Islands of Spanish Honduras). These settlements seem to have been purely for the purpose of extracting logwood and, later, mahogany, with perhaps a little buccaneering (which found an echo among their descendants in the days of prohibition in the United States). The distinction between a logwood-cutter and a buccaneer was perhaps rather uncertain. The Governor of Jamaica reported to Charles II that the settlement had 'increased His Majesty's Customs and the natural commerce more than any of His Majesty's Colonies'.

The settlement continued for 150 years with varying fortunes. There was intermittent strife with the Spaniards, irrespective of treaties between England and Spain regarding the area. The Spanish recognised the right of the settlers to cut timber, but prohibited the establishment of 'plantations'. There was thus no agricultural settlement. Belize could have been little more than a grandiose timber camp. Men, no doubt, came, made their fortunes and left. The less successful remained. Something of this characteristic remains in British Honduras today. During the 18th century slaves were imported, the first mention of them being in 1754. Slavery must have been a very much freer and looser institution than in the West Indies, as escape would be easy and the relations of master and slave were always good. In 1798, after the Battle of St George's Cay, when a Spanish invasion force was defeated, the permanent right of the settlers to the territory was established. There were then no restrictions on 'plantations', but this seems to have had little effect. What population there was would be required for the exploitation of the forests, which was more profitable than agriculture. The present Belize population seem to be largely the descendants of these settlers and their slaves. The rest of the country was settled from different sources in the 19th century.

In 1849 Spanish refugees from an Indian massacre in Mexico settled in the region round Corozal. A group of 'Caribs' (mixed Caribs and Negroes) from the West Indies were settled at Stann Creek and spread down the coast into Guatemala and Spanish Honduras. There is constant coming and going by sea between the different settlements of this people. In the latter part of the 19th century and in the present century Mayan Indian immigrants have settled in the interior from Guatemala. After the American Civil War, Confederates were settled in the south near Punta Gorda and imported East Indian labour to work their estates. Nearly all the descendants of these Americans have returned to the United States. These various groups have contributed to the present population of about 60,000, of whom about 20,000 live in Belize. It is a small population with which to develop the agricultural resources of the country, and the rewards of the forest are still greater than those of agriculture.

Historically the picture is one of continuous exploitation of the forest resources of the Colony with the sporadic settlement of small groups of agriculturists in the 19th century. It is almost a classic of colonial exploitation, of taking away and not giving back, with this difference, that there was no indigenous population whose resources were taken. Of all the wealth taken from the country practically nothing was put back in the way of permanent improvement and capital development. The disease which struck the banana industry left some settlements, such as Monkey River, stranded, able only to eke out a miserable existence on unsuitable land far from the village. A similar tale might have been told of the whole Colony, but that modern transport and machinery, tractors, great camions, bulldozers and so on, have enabled forests farther and farther from the rivers to be exploited until the operations reached over the border into Guatemala. The warning cry has gone up before of the exhaustion of the forest, but the evil day has been postponed. In 1892 the Governor addressed the Legislative Council in very modern terms, saying that the future of the Colony depended on agriculture and that settlers must be brought in.[1] It is interesting to follow the debates of Council from 1892 to 1897, when the project of a railway was under discussion. There is a certain comic element in the way that councillors were determined to have a railway, no matter where it went. They discussed all possible routes, but it is clear that what was moving them, in days before road transport had developed, was the need to open up parts of the forest which could not otherwise be reached. They rejected the already surveyed Belize River route to the west on the ground that the area had already been worked out. A survey up the Sibun River came back to report such a route impracticable. In the end a 'banana

[1] Sir Eric Swayne, in his address to the Royal Geographical Society in 1917, said much the same (*Geographical Journal*, vol. L, no. 3).

railway' up the Stann Creek valley was completed just as the banana industry entered its decline. It is now a road. The internal-combustion engine saved the mahogany industry.

The northern half of the Colony is almost all private land. The less accessible southern half is mainly Crown land. In the early days of mahogany extraction, freehold grants of large tracts of land, on a basis of so much river frontage and a depth of half-way to the next navigable stream were made for the exploitation of the forest resources. The possession of these tracts has become more concentrated in the course of time. Now the landlords, both absent and present, have not the interest in, nor the capital for, developing their lands. Nor is there the labour force to work them. No capital has been put into the land. Even the present-day investment of capital in machinery and plant for timber extraction is consumed in that extraction. When the tractors withdraw from an area the forest closes in and the roads which have been made return to their natural condition.

In recent years attempts have been made to reverse this situation. Roads are being built opening up new areas for agricultural development, and connecting up existing settlements with their markets. The cutting of timber is controlled on private land as well as Crown land. The Forest Department takes over some of the mahogany contractors' roads. A graduated land tax is being imposed to encourage development of good land.

Internationally the trade connections of the Colony have been mainly with the United States, Canada and the neighbouring republics. The reason for this is largely proximity. Much trade can be carried in small coasting vessels, whereas sea communications with the United Kingdom are poor. British Honduras has been a field for mainly American capital in recent years (capital of a short-term kind, as will appear later), and exports have returned to the source of the capital. Imports of machinery and consumers' goods, including food, have come from the same region. Most business connections are with the United States, especially New Orleans, and goods may be obtained more rapidly there than from Europe. A man importing machinery from the United Kingdom has to keep a large stock of spares, as there will be a long delay in replacement in the event of a breakdown. A man importing machinery from the United States can get replacements in a few days. If Belize were a worthwhile market, no doubt British suppliers would stock spares, at least in Jamaica. As it is, the Colony is, geographically, in the American economic orbit. A stricter exchange control in the last few years has succeeded in wrenching this pattern into a slightly different shape, at the expense of a lot of local frustration. In fact, the Colony is more dependent on the economy of the United States than on that of the United Kingdom. A token of this was the parity of the British Honduras and United States dollars which remained unchanged from 1894 until 1950.[1]

[1] See Note on the Devaluation of the British Honduras Dollar, p. 139.

III. SOURCES

The main sources used are set out below. Their detailed application will appear from the notes on the construction of the tables:

(*a*) *The 1946 Census*. The occupational classification in the Census was the backbone of the study and used for building up the major figures in the Output Table. Without it no table of any value could have been constructed, as there is no other information on the minor industrial groupings. Even so, the Census, taken in April, when the mahogany season was at its height and the chicle season had not begun, gave some serious distortions in the major groups, which had to be derived from other sources.

(*b*) *The Annual Financial Statements of the Colony*. These provided the most accurate figures used. From them were derived the share of government in the economy, both current and capital, the output of the business sector of government (although departments such as the supplies section of the Import Control Office were not included in them), certain figures of income received from abroad and interest paid abroad and the earnings of government employees.

(*c*) *The Customs Report*, giving details of imports and exports. The total Customs revenue collected, as shown in the Annual Financial Statements, differed from that shown in the Customs Report, as refunds were not deducted from the Customs figures. These refunds are partly on broken and damaged goods and short-shipments and partly on machinery, etc., for certain industries (mainly timber) refunded under the Customs Law on application by importers. The latter were used, together with imports admitted free in the first place, as a guide to the assessment of the amount of foreign capital invested in the Colony.

(*d*) *The Forest Department Report*. This is always a well-documented report and enabled certain cross-checks to be made in the forest industries. The figures, however, are not set out in a convenient way for national income studies.

(*e*) *The Labour Department Report and Notes by the Labour Officer on the preliminary Census returns.* The Report contains particulars of the numbers employed in the major industries (except agriculture) and some minor ones, with current wage rates. The Notes were produced before the Report and were an attempt to calculate the total earnings of different industries. They also provided some corrections to errors in the Census resulting from the time of year in which it was taken. Unfortunately there were considerable differences between the Notes and the Report and some arithmetical errors. Extension of the wage rates given in the Report, for the length of season given, sometimes produced obviously impossible results.

(*f*) *The Post Office Report* was used in arriving at figures of personal remittances.

(*g*) *The 1947 Agricultural Census*, prepared for the Evans Commission, was used as the main source for the output of agriculture. This was a census of the acreage under different crops and of the quantities of livestock. The Director of Agriculture had not great confidence in its accuracy but considered it a workable general picture, and as applicable to 1946 as to 1947. As it was the only source for agricultural output, it had, with a few minor adjustments recommended by the Director of Agriculture, to be treated as correct. It was used in conjunction with a similar census in 1943 for estimating the annual increase of livestock.

(*h*) *The 1947 Income Tax Report*, which relates to incomes for 1946, although in some cases the financial year of a concern taxed in 1947 would only end *some time* in 1946. This was not considered as unduly affecting the picture, as the economy did not undergo any marked changes between 1945 and 1947, such as would make necessary an adjustment in respect of the few firms concerned.

(*i*) *The Collector of Customs' Records of Fish sold in the Markets in 1948.* These records were prepared for the purpose of fisheries research into the catches of the various kinds of fish. For their purpose they were satisfactory, but required large adjustments for this study. It was assumed that activity in the internal fishing industry (as against the export industry) remained constant between 1946 and 1948.

(*j*) *The income tax assessments and the employers' returns of wages and salaries paid.* The latter are required to show only payments over $500 per annum. Some of them detail all wage payments. They cannot be used to arrive at a figure for the total number employed in an industry, as all employed are not included, and where all in a concern are included, there would be duplication of persons transferring from one concern or industry to another. They were chiefly used for making some judgments of the average earnings of different occupations. Such judgments were backed by personal knowledge derived from a large number of different sources. The income tax assessments for non-employees were all scrutinised. In only a few cases were detailed accounts submitted by firms. These provided useful information for checking other figures. The majority of the assessments, which relate to trade, were estimated for lack of accounts. This results in a large margin of error, as the assessments have the appearance of pure guesses. They differ so much from the figure returned by the taxpayer that one would assume that they greatly overestimated actual profits, were it not for the readiness with which the tax is paid, which suggests that they must, after all, be under-estimates. In fact, they are based on the assessor's judgment of the worth of a business, which can be fairly readily assessed in a small community, backed by his examination of such books of account as a business keeps, and its bank account. Other minor sources of information are acknowledged in the notes to the tables.

This summarises the main sources of information used. Some of it was available only after the inquiry had begun. It was the end of 1948 before it was all available. There are some obvious lacunae. The most noticeable was the lack of consumption studies, which would have provided a valuable check on the expenditure table and on the output of subsistence agriculture, which can only be checked by a study of the consumption habits of the persons concerned, as their products do not enter the market. It is unfortunate that the Colony has never been the subject of social or anthropological research, as the budgetary and dietary studies thrown out in the course of such enquiries would have been useful. The Labour Department made a survey of 100 working-class budgets in 1942, on which the official cost of living index is based. The results of this survey, as published in the Colony's *Annual Report*, indicate that in 1942 a working-class family spent $600 per annum, and to maintain that standard in 1946 would have to spend about $900 per annum. Yet the Labour Department's Report for 1946 suggests that average earnings were nearer $300 per annum. It would take nearly three earners in a household or family to provide the required income. The Census gives the average size of a household, including children and aged, as 4·363. It seemed wiser to ignore the survey.

There is no price index, so that adjustments to the tables from year to year cannot be made even with semblance of accuracy. The cost-of-living index, apart from its doubtful reliability, is confined to one class and differs quite appreciably from a cost-of-living index which I had occasion to prepare for a different and much smaller class, but one with wider spending habits. At the end will be set out certain proposals for collecting minimum statistics which would enable the tables to be drawn up annually.

There is no census of production. The Colony has concentrated its attention on exports only, with the result that the internal economy is largely undocumented and is only the object of policy in vague and unmeasured terms. For the successful development of the internal economy, especially agriculture, which is as vital to a large part of the community as exports are to other parts, some measurement of production is essential, something more than the general impression that, to quote the Agricultural Department's Report for 1946, 'in the northern district, the output of corn was ample', or 'the acreage planted to rice this year was almost double that of last year', without any indication of what an ample output of corn was or what the previous year's rice acreage was. The much-mooted change-over from a forest to an agricultural economy, which circumstances make pressing, is as important in its internal aspects (the lessening of imports and the increased variation of diet for health and welfare) as in its export aspects. It is probable that a dietetic study would suggest new lines for agricultural policy which, although perhaps small in money terms, would be of great importance to the health, welfare and productivity of labour.[1] For anything like this to be applied a more accurate measure of productivity will be needed. It is important in establishing an agricultural community to provide first for a stable and well-balanced internal economy before turning attention to exports, rather than establish a vulnerable community based on exports alone.

[1] 'The Medical Department recently reported that the diet of labourers while employed in forest operations is on the whole better than that of the labouring population generally. The protein consists of salted pork and beef, varied with fresh meat in the shape of game and birds; and beans. The carbohydrates are provided in the form of flour "dumplings" and rice, and fats in the form of lard and pork fat. The diet is somewhat deficient in fresh fruit and green vegetables. . . . The Colony is still largely dependent on outside sources for a large proportion of its food and the production of home foodstuffs would improve the conditions of health and nutrition through the eating of a properly balanced diet of fresh foodstuffs containing the essential elements for maintaining a healthy body' (*Annual Report on the Working of the Labour Department for the year ended 31st December 1948*).

IV. DEFINITIONS

The original intention was to draw up national income tables on a geographical basis, to show the net income due to the factors of production *operating* in the area described as British Honduras, irrespective of where the income went. This would have meant the inclusion of the profits of foreign-owned companies. By making certain adjustments it would then be possible to show the net income accruing to resident factors of production. The comparison of the two would be useful. In a dependent economy, where much of the activity is generated by outside capital, these two measures of the national income both have value and may be very different. Miss Deane used both in her study of Northern Rhodesia, except that she used the concept of 'taxable income' for the larger aggregate, which is not quite the same as the concept stated above, although in most cases it is identical. The peculiar structure of the British Honduras economy compelled the abandonment of the idea and the adoption of a definition of net national income accruing to normally resident factors of production. The taxable income concept was very suitable for the Northern Rhodesian economy, where a great part of the activity was financed by foreign capital and where the returns to that capital were known. In British Honduras there are only a very few foreign firms actually 'carrying on business' (in the income tax sense of the expression). The major trading concerns are locally owned with a few shareholders abroad. The concept of taxable income would thus yield figures very little different from the concept of net national income of residents. This does not mean that by any means all activity is locally financed. A large part of the timber production and all the chicle production are financed by foreign firms, mainly American, which are nominally only 'buying firms' in the Colony. These firms import capital in the form of machinery, cash and stores to a considerable sum, which they advance to local contractors who organise the extraction of timber and chicle. From the economic point of view they are investors, with a quick return of the total capital invested plus something extra. The equipment, etc., brought in has not a long life and might well be an item of expenditure in the firms' accounts, set off against receipts from the sale of timber. In normal times the inflow of equipment is steady and is the purchase price of timber and chicle. (Incidentally this must be much more than the declared value of exports and suggests under-valuation or incorrect measurement.) The profits of these firms, accruing as they do in the country of sale, are unknown and untaxed. As far as the Colony is concerned the firms are something more than simple buying firms. In other colonies buyers are obviously responsible for the prosperity of the industry from which they buy, but they do not provide the capital as well as buying the product. This sort of thing is, perhaps, only possible in timber-getting where the product of sixty years' growth is cut down and sold in a year, where a capital asset or an article which has taken sixty years to make can be had for the expense of getting it and sold for the expense of selling it. As the profits of these firms are not taxable they would not fall within the concept of taxable income, yet they are akin to the taxable profits of foreign-owned companies 'carrying on businesses' in other colonies. Their profits should be included in any estimate of the national income designed to show the net proceeds of all factors of production operating within the Colony. As their profits are unknown they cannot be included, and the concept has had to be dropped.

Net national income of normally resident factors of production is a *basic* concept. It has been modified in practice. The remittances of emigrants have been included and also interest and dividends received from abroad (except by Government). It seems more useful to include emigrants' remittances than exclude them, as many countries are great exporters of labour and the figure may be highly significant in a particular economy. Temporary emigrants (permanent ones are a wasting asset) should perhaps be considered as a foreign investment, although the return in remittances may be erratic and unforeseeable. If the emphasis is on output, as the total result of activities carried on in a given area, then their remittances would be excluded, as they are obviously part of the activity of the country to which the persons have emigrated. If the emphasis is on income and expenditure they will be included, as they increase the income and expenditure of the emigrant country and decrease those of the immigrant country. Considering national income tables as a summary of useful information, it is preferable to include them. For the same reason dividends and interest *received from* abroad are included. In some countries their effect on the economy is great, although this is not so in British Honduras. Interest and dividends *accruing* abroad to residents, but not received in the Colony by them, are excluded for the very simple reason that their amount is almost completely unknown, although they may be used to finance imports (especially under the restrictions of exchange control when they can pay for the importation of apparent 'gifts' from hard-currency sources). In theory this income accruing abroad has been made taxable in the last two years. In practice, except for a few honest men who return it, it is unknown and unknowable to the income tax authorities.

The definition 'resident' should be taken to mean normally resident and taxable. It will be seen below that the income of normal residents of British Honduras who cut timber or gather chicle over the border in Guatemala for quite long periods is treated as resident income. This may seem to be stretching the definition rather far, especially as the natural resources of British Honduras are not involved. It was not the original intention to include them, but it became necessary to import them into the tables if the Output Table was to balance the Expenditure Table, based as the latter was on imports. The men consume British Honduras imports and produce. Once included for balancing, they could easily be deducted from both tables, but it seemed justifiable to leave them in. Apart from firms which prefer to operate from British Honduras, as the most stable country in Central America, the forests over the

Guatemalan border are more accessible from the British Honduras side and provide easy access to the sea for logs floated down the Belize River. The workers go from British Honduras and return there; their supplies come from British Honduras. When, as at present, the border is closed, the men have to be absorbed by the British Honduras economy. As the extent of this activity over the border is of significance to the economy it should be included for informative purposes.

The treatment of some important specific items should be mentioned. The United Nations Statistical Office's list[1] is followed.

Unpaid services of housewives have not been included. This would be particularly difficult to estimate. If it is measured in terms of domestic servants' wages there is the curious result that in one home, with a good income, a wife would have several servants, and be assessed herself as equal to, say, a housekeeper; in a similar-sized home, with a small income and no servants, it might be necessary to assess the wife at the value of several servants. This is clearly common sense as the wife has more value (monetary) to the small-income husband than to the large, but it does not make assessment any easier. In fact, there is no base for estimating. The number of wives is known and the number of 'common law' wives is known, but many home-makers and mothers are single.[2] The figure would not have much significance except in a highly controlled society which needed to draw heavily on womanpower. In such a case the problem is more social than economic and the figures would probably already be available elsewhere. No unpaid services, of whatever kind, have been included, but their value has been used as a cross-check in agriculture.

Net rental of owner-occupied houses has been included.

Services of durable consumer goods have not been included.

Farmers' consumption of own produce has been included indirectly. This is an appreciable item in an economy with a

[1] *National Income Statistics, 1938-1947*, p. 8.

[2] The Census shows that there was in 1946 only one woman who had had twenty children, all of whom were still alive and, by reference to another table, that she was single!

large sector devoted to subsistence agriculture. The production of each crop has been estimated, valued at farm prices and the figure reduced for expenses (other than labour) to arrive at net output at the value to the farmer. This will include farmers' consumption of their own produce and also the free consumption by their labourers of their produce.

Payments in kind are included to the extent that they are included in income tax assessments of personal incomes. In theory these payments are taxable and included; in practice probably a fair number escape assessment. Where rations are paid in addition to wages an estimate of the value of the rations has been made and included in income.

Government services, civilian and military, are included, though not in total except in the expenditure table.

The income of armed forces abroad has not been included. No complete units (except a Forestry Unit) served abroad. The remittances of those serving with other armed forces were included. The income of the armed forces, local and foreign, serving in British Honduras was included. The basis has been actual residence. This illustrates the difficulty of dealing with a small dependent territory. In British Honduras there were armed forces consisting *mainly* of British Hondurans but paid for *mainly* by the United Kingdom. On this basis of residence one might find oneself in the position of having to exclude one's own forces and include an enemy occupation force. There may be logical grounds for this, but it is repugnant to feeling. In practice, the expenditure of the United Kingdom on the armed forces was included in the Colony's national income in so far as it generated personal incomes; it was excluded in so far as it generated imports.

Profits and losses of government-owned enterprises have been included when the accounts of the enterprise have been kept so as to reveal a profit or loss; in other cases the surplus or deficit only has been shown. Replacements of depreciated plant and new plant are met from revenue in the latter cases. It is necessary to make an assumption that replacements and new capital expenditure are steady, although this is not in fact so, in default of any knowledge of the present capital value of government concerns.

Profits of companies have been included before deducting dividends or companies' tax. This means, unfortunately, that the allocation of profits between dividends, investment and saving is masked.

Indirect taxes have been excluded and subsidies included in the expenditure table.

Interest on the national debt has not been included as it is almost entirely paid abroad. Interest on other public debt has been treated as transfer income as all other public debt is owed to the central government.

There were no deliveries under lend-lease or mutual aid, nor occupation costs nor reparations.

Remittances received by missions were included in so far as they generated incomes and excluded in so far as they generated imports.[1]

No adjustments for inventory revaluations were made as the information was not available. It is doubtful whether they would have any significance.

Stock market and real estate capital gains or losses are not included. There are no professional stockbrokers or real estate agents so that such capital gains or losses as are made by others are automatically excluded from figures derived from income tax sources.

Income is valued partly on a cash, partly on an accrual basis. The private sector is valued on an accrual basis (including agriculture). In many cases the cash and accrual basis will coincide. The government sector is valued on a cash basis (except for the supplies section of the Import Control Office). In agriculture account has been taken of the annual increase of (unsold) livestock, but not of stocks of produce on hand or crops in the ground.

[1] This treatment follows from the definition of national income. Remittances received by foreign missions, by foreign firms and by Government are considered as an export of goods and (labour) services to a foreign 'buyer'. The foreign 'buyer's' purchases of imports are of no real interest to the economy as it has been defined for the purpose of this study. See pp. 10-12.

There are no public social insurance or pension funds. Employers' and employees' contributions to pension funds have been treated as income of the employees. Medical services provided by Government free for indigent persons or at a nominal charge for low-income patients have been treated as part of the government expenditure on goods and services, and no income or expenditure has been imputed to consumers on that account.

Outdoor relief payments have been treated as transfer income and excluded.

Services rendered by banks and other financial intermediaries: no attempt has been made to impute to borrowers or lenders the value of services rendered without direct payment. The net value added by the banks has been taken to be the wages and salaries. Profit has been excluded as it accrues to non-resident factors of production. The bank was ignored as a redistributor of income by charging borrowers and paying lenders. The interest on the bank's property should be set against the profit and is not of local concern.

Commissions paid by individuals for transfer of securities and other property are included as income. They are mainly lawyers' fees. Bank charges on such transfers accrue in the same place as profits. The item is negligible in this context.

Illegal and immoral earnings are in theory excluded. The profits of smuggling are excluded, as being unknown and not unduly significant. This may be a false assumption in view of the long tradition of smuggling.

Depreciation and obsolescence have been allowed for at the usual income tax 'wear and tear' rates.

Allowances for bad debts are treated in the same way as by the income tax authorities.

The question of allowing for the depletion of the natural resources remains. Depletion occurs by overcutting of the forest, so that it cannot regenerate itself in the course of time or, better still, in the shortest natural course of time. When mahogany has been 'worked out' from an area where it is indigenous it will, no doubt, re-establish itself in time, although this may take much longer than might be the case if cutting were controlled. Where mahogany is not indigenous, overcutting might cause its complete disappearance. It is impossible to measure such nebulous ideas. In theory, all cutting is now controlled, on private as well as on Crown land, so that the cutting will be gradual and the forest allowed to regenerate itself in the shortest possible time. This control seems to be effective and it can, perhaps, be assumed that nowadays at least, there is, in fact, no depletion of the natural resources.

The losses caused by hurricanes which, though not regular, are frequent in one part of the Colony or another, and cause great damage to the forests[1], are considered to be a capital loss. They are not in any year a loss of income, so much as a potential loss of income. In fact, they may be an immediate source of income, as they may encourage the extraction of fallen timber in an area not being worked, without the expense of felling. If the losses were regular and measurable and greater than the replacement rate,[2] there might be some value in putting a negative element in the tables. If this were so, however, it is unlikely that there would be any marketable timber left now. It is sometimes said that those capital losses which are normally insured against should be deducted from gross income. The Government of British Honduras is formulating a hurricane insurance scheme, which would bring hurricane damage within such a principle. On the other hand, the Roman Catholics attribute the exemption of the Colony from hurricanes since 1945 to the annual procession held in honour of Our Lady of Guadelupe, instituted after that year. And this may be as good a system of insurance as the other.

If a true account were to be drawn up it would be necessary to have a national capital account as well as a national income

[1] 'The storm travelled from East to West and appears to have been about twenty miles wide from Monkey River mouth to the Sarstoon. It broke the leaves of the cohune palms but did not fell more than ten per cent; high forest in the centre of the storm was almost completely blown down' (*Report of the Forest Department, 1945*).

[2] 'The damage to the forest will take a hundred years to repair' (*Report of the Forest Department, 1946*).

account. The excess of cutting of timber over natural growth would have to be shown as a capital loss. This would entail an enumeration of the timber resources and an estimate of their natural annual increase. In turn it would entail estimating how much of this can be reached, cut and marketed; how much of a species which is cut in a special area is truly indigenous there and will regenerate itself; and many other factors which defy reasonably accurate measurement. A new invention, made in another part of the world, such as the internal-combustion engine, which increases the area of exploitable timber, would increase the value of the national capital. While round-figure estimates can no doubt be made by experts, the figures would be so round as to have little practical value. This is the problem of a capital account in the setting of a forest economy. It arises elsewhere in mining economies where it is equally intractable. In so far as minerals do not reproduce themselves the matter is simpler. But the existence of any given mineral area as an asset in one's capital account might depend on the market price of the mineral. If this fell below a certain figure, the area might be uneconomic to work, and the asset would have no value; a rise in price would bring it back into account. It would be an interesting exercise to try to measure these things, but not valuable, as all that one desires to know is whether one is living on capital or not and how much longer the capital will last. These primary facts are generally known, and to try to assess them year by year, to value and re-value them, would add little to one's knowledge. The money notation used in national income studies has no significance of its own; it is simply the easiest way of measuring and comparing the income, output and expenditure of different sectors of the economy. A comparison of one year with another (when the value of money has changed) is only significant in so far as the shares of each sector vary.

V. STRUCTURE OF THE TABLES

Ideally the three tables of Income, Output and Expenditure should be separately estimated. Miss Deane found that this was not wholly practicable for the three colonies which she studied, owing to the paucity of source-material. This paucity of material was even more marked in British Honduras and permitted only a few cross-checks at some critical points which enabled the general picture to be wrenched into more accurate shape. I have had, through access to unpublished information in the hands of Government and three years' personal experience in the Colony, more detail on some parts of the economy than might have been expected, which has strengthened the figures considerably, only to be met by a complete lack of information on others. The blank parts of the economy have been filled in on the basis of inferences made from experience and conversations with those acquainted with those parts. The figures thus express only some impressions gained. The final figures must be regarded as tentative. They are theoretically capable of almost infinite refinement in detail, by correcting the detail and improving the assumptions. Nevertheless, I would not expect any appreciable alterations in the totals nor in the figures of the major groupings.

One of the difficulties of dealing with a very small economy is that factors which are quite small and relatively insignificant in a large economy take on a greater importance. Handicrafts may play a small part in an industrialised economy but a large part in a primitive one. Whereas in a larger economy these smaller factors can be dealt with by fairly general assumptions, in a small economy they need more careful treatment. The activities of individuals, rather than of groups and industries, have to be measured.

The main table is the Output Table. For Agriculture it has been based very loosely and with a large margin of error on output. Only the very roughest cross-check was available on an income basis. For other industries it has been based on earnings of employees and profits of employers or own-account workers. This gives the net value added. Cross-checks of a fairly close kind were available when dealing with Timber-getting, Sugar-growing, Sawmilling and Fishing.

The Income Table is a rearrangement of the items in the Output Table. As many of the subdivisions as possible were independently arrived at, but there remained two very large residual items which could only be checked by the broadest inferences. The total has little validity of its own. Nevertheless, the table has been used to recheck the Output Table at one or two points.

The Expenditure Table, which could not be built up independently from analyses of expenditure, as there were none, is based on domestic imports plus the value of domestic output not exported. This provides a useful check on the output of the export industries as they, after taking into account the invisible items in the Balance of Payments, have to meet the expenditure on imports. It does not, of course, give any check on those figures in the Output Table which deal with output for domestic consumption, as these figures are themselves used for constructing the Expenditure Table.

Government income received from abroad and the investments of foreign companies has been included in the tables in so far as they generate incomes, but excluded in so far as they generate imports. Imports generated by foreign funds are not considered as part of the national income as they are not the result of activities within the Colony. Incomes generated by foreign funds are part of the Colony's activities.

It would be unreal to put specific figures in for the margins of error, which would be highly subjective and no more than an expression of my own opinion of how accurate a given figure is. I have tried to indicate in general terms where a figure is fairly accurate or a broad approximation. Generally this will be self-evident from the notes.

VI. INCOME TABLE AND NOTES

Income, 1946

	$000	$000	$000
1. *Profits from Estates:*			
From Income Tax Report .			90
2. *Profits from Trade, Business or Profession:*			
From Income Tax Report (less profits not due to resident factors of production) . . .		1,560	
plus not assessed . . .		9	
plus Government surpluses and profits on trading services:			
Post and Telegraphs . .	64		
Electricity and Telephones .	22		
School Supplies Store . .	2		
Import Control . . .	80		
	168		
less deficit:			
Board of Agriculture . .	2	166	
		1,735	
less rents and royalties:			
Agricultural rents . .	75		
Private forest royalties .	70	145	
			1,590
3. *Earnings of Farmers, Tradesmen and Small Shopkeepers working on own account:*			
6827 @ $500			3,414
Carry forward .			5,094

	$000	$000	$000
Brought forward .			5,094
4. *Salary-Earners* (797):			
From Income Tax Report . .			1,397
5. *Wage-Earners:*			
10,559 @ $290 . . .			3,062
6. *Interest:*			
Interest and dividends from abroad		90	
Local interest		7	
		——	97
7. *Rents, Royalties, etc.:*			
From Income Tax Report . .		52	
Government		107	
Agricultural rents . . .		75	
Private timber royalties . .		70	
Housing: imputed net rents .	668		
less Income Tax Report . .	52		
	——	616	
		——	920
8. *Remittances from Abroad:*			
From Postal Report and various government accounts . .			237
			——
			10,807

The Income Table is the weakest of the three. It purports to show, for example, that the incomes of *x* wage-earners were so much per annum and that the incomes of *y* workers on their own account were so much more per annum. These, the largest constituents of the table, are really a division of a residual figure as a result of the rearrangement of the figures in the Output Table. Neither the Census nor any other information allowed a more precise breakdown. The Census was taken in April when the timber industry was in full swing and the chicle industry in its off-season. It is known from the Forest Department's chicle licences that over a thousand more persons found employment in the chicle industry during the year than are shown in the Census. The seasonal factor in work is one of the most significant features of the Colony's economy. A man reaps his crop, goes out and collects chicle in the forest, returns to plant his *milpa* and may then find employment in agriculture, timber or elsewhere. This interchange occurs throughout the primary industries of the Colony. The secondary and tertiary industries are more stable. Although the Census attempts to enumerate subsidiary agriculturists and subsidiary fishermen and for those enumerated gives their chief occupation, it does not enumerate subsidiary forest workers. Indeed it is probably impossible to say in many cases that one industry is subsidiary to another. Any definition under that head is probably a subjective one, as much based on what the person was doing at the time of the Census, or his personal tastes and preferences, as anything else. The same point arises between workers on their own account and wage-earners. A man may, in one year, be a worker on his own account in agriculture, a wage-earner in agriculture, a contractor in chicle-getting and a wage-earner in timber-getting, even if he does not vary his employment with fishing as well. The distinction between wage-earners and own-account workers is unreal, although the figures for the two groups probably give a fair indication of the relative amounts of work done on own account and in employment.

I. PROFITS FROM ESTATES

This figure is taken from the Income Tax Report. It is probable that some estates' profits escape assessment, as there is no ready means of checking profits returned when no accounts are furnished, as there are with businesses. There are also, however, some estate losses which are not deducted from the income tax figure. It has been assumed that the losses are equivalent to the unassessed profits. The figure is probably fairly accurate. It may appear low in a country the size of British Honduras, but that is because the large estates in private hands are held for the exploitation of timber and chicle. Only small parts, if any, of the estates are cultivated by the owners or by anyone with the capital to employ labour. The bulk of the agriculture is in the hands of peasant farmers either renting their land from estate owners or government, or working their own land.[1]

2. PROFITS FROM TRADE, BUSINESS OR PROFESSION

This figure is taken from the Income Tax Report, less profits not due to resident factors of production, plus a residual figure of $9000 to cover unassessed profits. Surpluses of government trading services less government trading losses, plus the profits of the supplies section of the Import Control Office have been added. $75,000 estimated agricultural rents and $70,000 estimated private royalties have been deducted. These last two items are independently estimated and are greater than the Income Tax Report figure for rents. They have been deducted here on the assumption that the excess is included in the generalised, estimated, income tax assessments of trade profits. The error is unlikely to be large.

3. EARNINGS OF FARMERS, TRADESMEN AND SMALL SHOPKEEPERS WORKING ON OWN ACCOUNT

This class of person is a large proportion of the Colony's gainfully-occupied population, but, as has been shown, in many cases there is no real distinction between this class and wage-earners, as far as the primary industries as a whole are concerned. The Census gives 362 employers and 6900 own-account workers, a total of 7262.

The Income Tax Report showed that 435 employers, etc., had been assessed, leaving 6827 unassessed own-account workers. Their average income has been estimated at $500 per annum. This is based on several assumptions and personal inferences. The employers' returns of wages give some indication

[1] 'The bulk of the food crops are produced by numerous small individual planters who perform the labour themselves and may employ one or two hands casually to assist them. Large estate plantations are few, and with the exception of these it is difficult to obtain any statistics of the numbers employed' (*Annual Report on the Working of the Labour Department for the year ended 31st December 1949*).

of the earnings of employed tradesmen. The income tax allowances for a married man with two children are $1000. It might be assumed that $700 was a reasonable estimate for the unassessed class. This, however, has to be reduced to account for the small farmers, subsistence agriculturists and others who are of no interest to the Income Tax Department, and for the childless and unmarried. The figure of $500 seems the highest that can be attributed to this class as an average. Reference to the item 'Agriculture', in the Output Table, where an attempt has been made to put a very rough check on the output of agriculture by means of estimated average incomes, suggests that $300 per annum should be the agricultural own-account workers' average. This would leave an average of $700 per annum for other than agricultural own-account workers. The latter figure may seem low by Belize standards, but it includes the districts where work and business will not be so plentiful (nor basic expenditure so high).[1] The margin of error in what is part of a residual figure is, therefore, not as high as might be expected.

[1] It may seem as though a figure *b* is being derived from figure *a* and then being used to check figure *a*; that the Output Table, including the item 'Agriculture', is used to check the Income Table, and produce the item 'Own-account workers', which is then used to check the item 'Agriculture', which is then used to check the item 'Own-account workers'. It is not quite as bad as that. Actually the figure for 'Agriculture' is independently estimated. It is then used with a large number of other figures to produce the item 'Own-account workers' (which can be lightly checked independently), so that the latter figure is only the result of the estimate of 'Agriculture' in respect of a small fraction. The check on the item 'Agriculture' is then made by taking the lowest possible figures for wage-earners and own-account workers (assuming that the latter earn more than the former or they would not continue working on their own account), as lower would be below subsistence level, and adding the value of unpaid help. The accuracy of this 'lowest' figure is then checked by deducting agricultural own-account workers from the total 'Own-account workers', which leaves an income for other own-account workers of $700, which is what was originally estimated on other grounds:

4151 @ $300 = $1,245,300 agricultural
2676 @ $700 = $1,873,200 other
$3,118,500

This division is, however, the result of too many extensions of estimated figures to be worth putting in the table.

4. SALARY-EARNERS

The figure shown in the Income Tax Report for assessed incomes from employment, which covers 769 persons, has been treated as the income of salary-earners. On this definition the margin of error is slight. The definition is not valid today, as increases in wages have brought a number of wage-earners up to taxable levels.

5. WAGE-EARNERS

Other employees (i.e. non-assessed) are treated as wage-earners. The Census showed that the gainfully occupied population was 20,133, of whom wage- and salary-earners totalled 12,007, of whom 11,058 were at work (including learners) and 949 were unemployed.[1] Deducting the 769 classed as salary-earners leaves 10,289, to which has to be added 270 forest workers estimated at work over the border at the time of the Census.[2] The average income has been assessed at $290 per annum, an inference made from wage rates shown in the Labour Report to yield $3,062,000. The figure for unemployed is assumed to refer to casual, temporary and seasonal unemployment and to be more or less constant throughout the year. The labour force is extremely mobile between jobs, and the general attitude to employment is such that a man might be technically unemployed at the time of the Census and yet not 'unemployed' in the generally accepted sense. He may even have earned enough, in his opinion, to warrant a rest. He may be doing what he regards as subsidiary work at the time. In spite of an unemployment ratio of nearly 8 per cent there does not seem to have been any unemployment 'problem' in 1946. In a small population with highly seasonal industries there may be an

[1] 'The problem however is mainly one of under-employment as the majority of workers—save a small percentage of unemployables—are able to secure some employment in the course of a month, their earnings however being altogether inadequate to enable them to provide for themselves and their families' (*Annual Report on the Working of the Labour Department for the year ended 31st December 1947*).

[2] '238 persons were known to be absent in Guatemala at the time of the Census and to be engaged there in mahogany cutting' (*Census of British Honduras, 1946*, chap. VII, para. 14).

absolute figure for unemployment below which the economy would cease to function properly through a shortage of labour. (This point may be of significance in certain localities of much more highly developed economies. The minimum practicable unemployment must vary from place to place with the economic structure and the density of population.)

6. INTEREST

A figure of $40,000 as the estimated income and dividends received from abroad was based on information obtained by the Financial Secretary, plus $50,000 of Government Savings Bank interest from abroad. $7000 was added for local interest, based on a scrutiny of the income tax returns. No local dividends are included here, as profits have been shown under item 2 before payment of dividends. Interest, on the other hand, is deducted in arriving at profits. To show local dividends here would be misleading, as it is quite impossible to show the drawings from proprietary firms, which form by far the greater part of the locally-owned concerns. To separate dividends, with the implication that profits under item 2 were retained profits, would give a false impression.

7. RENTS, ROYALTIES, ETC.

The Income Tax Report figure was first taken. The rents and royalties of government, from the Colony's accounts, were added. An imputed net annual value was given to housing in towns by taking the yields of property tax in towns and multiplying by the appropriate figure in each case for the rate of tax to arrive at the annual rental value of the property. This gave the following results:

Belize	$700,000
Corozal	30,000
Orange Walk	14,000
Stann Creek	70,000
Punta Gorda	16,000
Monkey River	5,000
	$835,000

The annual value for property tax purposes is probably considerably lower than the actual returns from rents, so that, although the maintenance and repair of wooden houses is extremely expensive, it was considered sufficient to deduct 20 per cent to arrive at the net imputed rental. From the resultant figure was deducted the $52,000 appearing in the Income Tax Report, on the assumption that it was included in the imputed rent. In fact, of course, some of it would cover agricultural rent and forest royalty. It was assumed that agricultural rents on the more thickly populated private lands of the north would be approximately double those on the Crown lands of the south. It was also assumed that private forest royalties would be rather less than government royalties as so much timber has already been 'worked out' on the private lands. No attempt was made to estimate agricultural housing, which, for most of the agricultural population, is of the pole-and-thatch type with a short life.

8. REMITTANCES FROM ABROAD

This figure is the value of foreign money and postal orders cashed in the Colony and remittances paid through various government accounts. At that time numbers of emigrant workers were employed in Panama and the U.S.A. while many were still with the forces abroad.[1] Included are the recipients of imperial pensions. It was assumed that money and postal orders bought were not for unrequited remittances but, more likely, for the purchase of imports. It was also assumed that orders paid in the Colony were for remittances, as it was unlikely that any would be for the purchase of exports. The

[1] 'The number of British Hondurans employed in the U.S.A. . . . diminished gradually throughout the year and by the 31st December the number of natives of this Colony remaining in that country was 167. . . . The employment available in the Canal Zone was reduced considerably. . . . The number of workers now in that area . . . is estimated not to exceed 100 . . . of the British Honduras Forest Unit . . . a balance of 335 . . . have not yet returned, the majority of whom are believed to be still in the United Kingdom' (*Annual Report on the Working of the Labour Department for the year ended 31st December 1946*).

figure includes only amounts which increase personal income. Remittances through the bank for the account of government or foreign firms, which are unrequited by exports, are estimated separately under 'Government Receipts from Abroad' and 'Investment by Foreign Companies' and deducted from the Expenditure Table.

VII. OUTPUT TABLE AND NOTES

Output, 1946

% of *National Income*		$000	$000
	1. *Agriculture:*		
1·79	(*a*) Maize	194	
0·80	(*b*) Rice	86	
0·23	(*c*) Beans and peas . . .	24	
1·26	(*d*) Ground provisions and root crops	137	
0·23	(*e*) Vegetables . . .	24	
0·57	(*f*) Bananas	61	
0·18	(*g*) Plantains	18	
1·52	(*h*) Grapefruit and tinned juice	164	
0·09	(*i*) Oranges	6	
0·01	(*j*) Other citrus . . .	1	
3·08	(*k*) Coconuts	333	
0·02	(*l*) Pineapples . . .	3	
1·47	(*m*) Cattle	157	
0·02	(*n*) Sheep and goats . .	2	
0·98	(*o*) Pigs	106	
1·11	(*p*) Poultry	120	
0·21	(*q*) Alligator skins . . .	23	
0·05	(*r*) Cohune	6	
0·89	(*s*) Sugar	96	
0·47	(*t*) Other crops . . .	50	
			1,611
	2. *Quarrying*		3
	3. *Fishing*		110
	Carry forward . .		1,724

% of National Income		$000	$000
	Brought forward .		1,724
	4. *Forestry:*		
11·65	(*a*) Timber-getting and sawmilling	1,253	
0·29	(*b*) Firewood	31	
9·29	(*c*) Chicle-bleeding . .	1,000	
0·15	(*d*) Forest cultivation . .	16	
		——	2,300
	5. *Manufacturing and Repair:*		
1·01	(*a*) Food	108	
0·63	(*b*) Beverages . . .	68	
0·37	(*c*) Tobacco	40	
0·02	(*d*) Oils and fats . . .	3	
0·15	(*e*) Chemicals . . .	16	
0·68	(*f*) Wood and cork (not sawmilling) . . .	75	
0·47	(*g*) Paper, printing and photography	51	
0·03	(*h*) Leather	4	
2·59	(*i*) Apparel, textile articles .	278	
0·66	(*j*) Electricity and water . .	70	
0·01	(*k*) Non-metallic minerals .	1	
0·21	(*l*) Metal manufacture . .	23	
2·20	(*m*) Machinery and vehicles .	235	
0·17	(*n*) Instruments, jewellery and other	18	
		——	990
	6. *Construction:*		
3·48	(*a*) Building	373	
1·92	(*b*) Road	207	
0·05	(*c*) Other construction . .	6	
		——	586
	Carry forward . .		5,600

% of National Income		$000	$000
	Brought forward .		5,600
	7. *Transport and Communications:*		
0·02	(*a*) Rail	2	
1·36	(*b*) Motor	146	
0·19	(*c*) Other road transport . .	21	
2·45	(*d*) Water	263	
0·25	(*e*) Air	27	
0·90	(*f*) Communications . .	97	
		—	556
	8. *Commerce:*		
14·34	(*a*) Retail and wholesale trade .	1,542	
1·03	(*b*) Finance	111	
		—	1,653
	9. *Recreational Service:*		
0·33	(*a*) Cinemas	35	
0·10	(*b*) Other	11	
		—	46
	10. *Professional Service:*		
2·00	(*a*) Medical and hygiene . .	215	
0·07	(*b*) Undertaking, cemetery and other hygiene . .	8	
1·35	(*c*) Education . . .	145	
0·68	(*d*) Religion	73	
		—	441
	11. *Public Service:*		
3·69	(*a*) Armed Forces . . .	396	
3·20	(*b*) Administration . . .	345	
0·38	(*c*) Law	41	
1·16	(*d*) Police, prisons . . .	125	
		—	907
	Carry forward . .		9,203

% of National Income		$000	$000
	Brought forward . .		9,203
	12. *Personal Service:*		
0·89	(*a*) Hotels, restaurants and cafés	96	
0·44	(*b*) Laundry, dry cleaning .	48	
0·18	(*c*) Hairdressing . . .	19	
1·29	(*d*) Domestic service . .	139	
			302
2·84	13. *Odd Jobs* (ill-defined industries) .		307
6·18	14. *Housing*		668
3·03	15. *Income from Abroad* . . .		327
			10,807

The Output Table is the strongest of the three. Apart from the primary industries it is based on the Census, on the assumption that employment in secondary and tertiary industries is steady and less subject to change. With these industries output has been calculated by taking the profits of employers and the earnings of employees. In Fishing and Forestry and certain minor items both income and output calculations were possible. Agriculture can only be lightly checked from the income side. The categories of the Census have been followed closely. As a result only a part of the activities of Government are shown separately (their total effect appears in the Expenditure Table).

Some of the classifications are a little uncertain. For example, under Transport and Communications the output of transport which derives directly from any other industry has generally been included under that industry and not under Transport. It is clear, however, that the Census classification is the result of some arbitrary decisions on the part of the persons concerned. Two employees appear under Railways. The railway in question is a logging railway owned by a private firm and either these two should come under Timber-getting or all other employees connected with it should come under Railways and a profit be imputed to it. Similarly, construction which belongs to a particular industry, and is part of its wage bill, is generally included under it and not under Construction. The detailed figures make only a pretence at accuracy and in their lesser subdivisions should be regarded with suspicion, at least. At the end of the Output Table appears a large unallocated item which might well wreck any of the smaller divisions if it could be distributed. It is obvious, too, that under Motor Vehicle Bodies there cannot be three employees and no employer. The rest of the output under this heading comes elsewhere, where the employers' profits are included, and may not even come under the general head of Manufacturing and Repair. These details are only used as a means of building up totals in the large groups. They have small validity on their own. As a means to their end they are useful. The larger groups probably do not err widely.

Considerable use has been made of income tax assessments in arriving at profit figures. Where only one concern occurs in any subdivision the calculation cannot, of course, be given, but profits and earnings are combined. Earnings of employees have generally been derived from inferences drawn from employers' returns of employees' wages, income tax assessments and the Labour Report. In particular cases information derived from other sources has been used.

I. AGRICULTURE

The Colony is generally thought of as non-agricultural. As far as trade statistics go this is true. Agricultural exports are slight compared with forest exports, and imports are considerable. Only a third of the food consumed is locally produced. Nevertheless the settlement of the 19th century was mainly agricultural and, in 1946, 29·13 per cent of the gainfully-occupied population found employment in agriculture. A large part of them are subsistence or near-subsistence agriculturists. Where there are means of communication, parts of the crop find their way to market. With the building of roads the agricultural potential of the present population, most of which meets only the personal needs of the grower, should be fully utilised.[1] A Board of Agriculture has for many years maintained minimum prices for maize, rice and beans and has bought up surplus supplies beyond those which can be marketed directly by the farmer at more favourable prices and those needed for his own storage and seed. During the war production was encouraged by a hortatory campaign and the itinerant services of farm demonstrators aiming at improving agricultural methods. These seem to have been based on the mixed peasant farming[2] recommendations of the *West India Commission Report* of 1939, now superseded by the large-scale production methods proposed in the *Evans Commission Report*. In 1948 the Board of Agriculture was converted into a Marketing Board with the idea of giving some positive stimulus to agricultural production. At the time of writing, apart from some romantic ideas of tractor, etc., stations in different parts of the Colony, the new Board does not yet seem to have formulated its policy. It has, however,

[1] 'Growers supplying isolated communities have developed the habit of withholding supplies in order to maintain artificially high prices. Such a policy . . . has led to the neglect of many local products because an imported substitute has been found to be just as cheap or cheaper. . . . This shortsighted policy has resulted in the maintenance over the past three years of a high level of imports of foodstuffs, much of which could have been produced here. . . . It is hoped that the feeder road programme, by tapping larger agricultural areas, may help to create a freer flow of locally grown foodstuffs at competitive rates' (*Department of Agriculture Annual Report for 1948*).

[2] 'One of the most striking features of the agriculture of the Colony is the lack of a knowledge of the elementary principles of good husbandry by the bulk of the small cultivators. . . . A comparatively large staff of practical well-trained demonstrators is needed. . . . It is felt that the self-sufficient small farm of the future must be based upon a system of "mixed farming"' (*Department of Agriculture Annual Report for 1944*).

'If any substantial increase in the volume of production for the home market is to be secured, it is evident that this must come mainly from agriculture. For this purpose, we believe that the substitution, wherever possible, of mixed farming methods for the single crop system of agriculture now predominant in the West Indies and the extension of peasant agriculture along appropriate lines will be required' (*West India Commission Report*, chap. III, para. 22).

enormously extended the practice of giving advances of cash and seed to farmers, after a minimum acreage has been cleared and before planting. This is an extension of the advance system, common in the forest industry, to agriculture. In fact, this is the traditional way of setting labour in motion in the Colony.[1] Whereas, however, with labour an advance can be recovered by a given amount of labour performed, in agriculture the return can never be certain. In a bad year, such as 1949, when a prolonged drought ruined the harvest, most of the loans would have to be written off and the policy may become expensive. It remains to be seen whether it will stimulate agriculture or merely increase a bad habit. Clearly, however, there can be no settlement of new agriculturists unless they are supplied with initial capital. As it is, loans are only made to established farmers, and it is probably safe to say that most of the population which is likely to be successful in agriculture is already engaged in it. This, coupled with over-population of the West Indies, has naturally stimulated thoughts of settlement from elsewhere, as it did fifty years ago, and has culminated in the Evans Commission, which made extensive suggestions for agricultural development. There is, nevertheless, an agricultural population in the Colony already, whose potential output is far from being reached. Improved methods,[2] improved communications and assured markets should, by themselves, enormously increase production. Unfortunately the Marketing Board, which provides the assured market for the farmers, is not always able to find an assured market for itself. Production of a crop which does not meet domestic requirements can always be protected, but the domestic market is really small,

[1] 'The mahogany cutters . . . used to sell themselves into a sort of slavery by receiving advances from their employers at the beginning of the season, which advances they spent most liberally in the town . . . leaving their families to starve' ('British Honduras', an address by Sir Eric Swayne in 1917 (discussion): *Geographical Journal*, vol. L, no. 3). A rather melodramatic description!

[2] 'The lack of any permanent application to agriculture has resulted over most of the Colony in a complete absence of farm tools and equipment. The implements in universal use are the axe and the machete' (*Department of Agriculture Annual Report for 1947*).

and in 1948 the Board exported surplus maize—at a loss. This was because local prices were rather higher than elsewhere.

This is, perhaps, the crucial weakness of any proposals for developing agriculture. The Colony has grown by its forest industries from which it has paid for imported food. The latter has been expensive (and is subject to import duty) and earnings in the forest industries have been high by Caribbean standards.[1] As long as the local demand for any produce is not exceeded by the local supply, the price will be as high for local produce as for imported produce.[2] This raises the return to agricultural work and makes it comparable with forest work. It effectively prohibits the development of agricultural exports, as at prices offered for exports there is no incentive to produce any surplus to subsistence needs.[3] The Mayan Indian and Spanish-Indian plants his *milpa* (the 'plot' of shifting cultivation), which will supply him with his basic food needs of the year, and will then go off to the forest and earn anything from $200 to $3000 collecting chicle, or he will work in the cane fields, earning about $1.50 a day. As long as he can get such returns from other work he will not waste his time planting more corn. It is interesting to note that the record corn harvest of 1948 coincided with a falling off in chicle operations, the price offered for chicle being much lower than in former years. The para-

[1] 'The total area of the Colony is 8,600 square miles, of which only approximately 60,000 to 70,000 acres have been cultivated or used for agriculture in any one year. For the remainder the relatively small population have worked it over for various forest products which have enabled them to maintain a relatively high standard of living in the past. . . . Agricultural development has run up against two major problems as a result in the past. The first problem has been that of the high cost of labour in comparison with labour of similar quality in purely agricultural countries. The second problem has been the almost complete absence of road transport and therefore the development of parochialism in local tastes and demand for agricultutal produce' (*Department of Agriculture Annual Report for 1948*).

[2] Fresh tomatoes from the United States, carefully graded, in perfect condition, packed in 1-lb. boxes and covered with cellophane, sell at the same or lower prices than locally grown tomatoes of inferior quality.

[3] The Corozal Sugar Factory in the 1948-9 season exported a small quantity of sugar, at a price lower than the domestic price. It yielded a slight profit. But if the whole output had been sold at that price there would have been little or no profit.

mount need in agricultural development is to lower nominal wages throughout the Colony, without, of course, lowering real wages, which are none too high. Otherwise the Colony's wages-prices structure will be too high to allow it to compete with the rest of the world in agricultural production. This consideration applies equally to any schemes for importing settlers as it does to the agriculturists already in the Colony. The ways of achieving this would seem to be by:

(*a*) improving communications so that more subsistence settlements could be brought within reach of the market and untapped areas could be made available;

(*b*) encouraging the use of more and more advanced tools and the more careful selection of seed [1] (it is doubtful if the southern half of the Colony can ever make *extensive* use of machinery), in order to increase production with the same manpower; [2]

(*c*) assuring a steady market, which might mean diversifying crops rather than increasing one crop once the home market had been filled; [3] and

(*d*) doing everything to reduce the high wages-prices structure (such as reducing or abandoning the duty on imported foods which do not compete with domestic production).

Devaluation of the British Honduras dollar, for example, would have the immediate effect of raising the working-class cost of living greatly, and soon wage-rates. This would encourage people to desert agriculture for wage-earning (always assuming that the wage-earning industries could bear the cost of the increases). Any temporary advantage for exports would soon be

[1] Rice is reaped with penknives on a selective method, as the grain grows unevenly and ripens irregularly. See *Department of Agriculture Annual Report for 1945*.

[2] But 'The wider use of such implements of cultivation is only likely where the farmer owns his land. The high cost of stumping and lack of security of tenure limit their use on farms which are rented. On these lands, for the same reason, growers hesitate to cultivate long-term crops or adopt any system of crop rotation' (*Department of Agriculture Annual Report for 1947*).

[3] It is in this, through the discriminate fixing of prices, that the Marketing Board might find its most useful function, and be a direct expression of agricultural policy.

nullified, and, anyway, at the moment exports are not the prime need of agricultural development. The wages-prices structure would be raised instead of lowered and make future exports quite impossible.[1]

The output of agriculture proved to be the most intractable item in the table. Hopes that the confidential Mayan Indian Report would yield some facts about the Indians, which could be used in measuring their output, were disappointed. All its facts were derived from other (known) sources. Its opinions did not differ much from the opinions which any person of fair intelligence might hold, having visited the Indian villages. Neither production nor consumption has been studied for any of the particular agricultural groups. All the experts who visit the Colony in increasing numbers, for a week each, make the routine visit to the Indian village of San Antonio in the Toledo district, where they spend a few hours. But they seek information rather than provide it. In parenthesis it might be added that the money spent on bringing the experts to the Colony to acquire the very scanty information available might be better spent on actual studies to produce more information.[2]

In the event the basis of the figure for Agriculture was the acreage census made by the Department of Agriculture for the Evans Commission in 1947. The calculations were worked out in collaboration with the Director of Agriculture and the assumptions made were based on his judgment. The principle adopted was to take the acreage given in the census for each crop, multiply this by an estimated figure for average yield and again by the price paid to the farmer by the middleman or received direct by the farmer (according to whether he marketed his crop directly or indirectly), and deduct a varying percentage for cost of materials used, seed and transport costs to market.

[1] See Note on the Devaluation of the British Honduras Dollar, p. 139.

[2] An interesting commentary on this is provided by the two experts who, as a result of faulty data, produced conflicting theories on the prospects of supplying Belize with water from the pine ridge eleven miles away. The argument continued, with Government convinced now by one, now by the other, until a third arrived who went to look at the borehole which supplied the data and found that the strata revealed by it had been incorrectly described.

(The percentage was varied to reflect the proportion of a crop marketed and the proportion consumed or sold on the farm.) The yield figures are uncertain, but are based on the best opinion available.

In finding the prices for 1946, Mr H. E. C. Cain kindly conducted some inquiries among middlemen and producers on my behalf. Prices varied considerably during the year, especially for coconuts, which ranged from $180 to $30 per 1000. As far as possible prices at the height of a crop season were taken, since the bulk of the crop would be sold then and crops not marketed would fetch the lowest prices on farms. The earnings of farmers would depend again on whether they carried their own crops to market or hired transport, or sold them on the spot to middlemen who provided transport. The Board of Agriculture provided free transport from its buying centres, except for corn, for which it set a lower price in the districts than in Belize. With livestock, attempts were made to estimate the slaughterings from the livestock figures in the census, by estimating the natural increase and deaths and so arriving at a balance. The balance was then reduced by comparing the 1947 census with a similar one in 1943 and estimating the annual increase of stock on farms. A large proportion of the slaughterings would not take place at municipal slaughter-houses.

A very rough check can be put on the total for Agriculture from the income side, using the Census figures for the numbers engaged in agriculture.

	$
Profits from estates	90,000
4151 own-account workers, etc., @ $300 .	1,245,300
592 unpaid helpers, valued @ $125 . .	74,000
1010 employees @ $200	202,000
	1,611,300

Profits and earnings of subsidiary cultivators have not been included specifically. The larger ones will be included under Profits from Estates, the lesser ones are not likely to be included in the agricultural census. The implication is that the figure for Agriculture has not been over-estimated, although it is surprisingly high.

(*a*) *Maize*. Corn is grown from north to south, chiefly by the Mayan Indians. The production in the north comes mainly from the area between the Hondo and New Rivers. This area supplies the greater part of the surplus for the market, but has to bear most of the competition for the *milpero's* interest from chicle. The system of agriculture is primitive in the south and west, the 'shifting cultivation' of large parts of Central Africa. The bush is burnt and the seed planted in holes made with sticks. There the villages occur in broken country and the corn has to be planted on slopes, sometimes incredibly steep ones, for there is little available flat land. Steep hills are planted to the summits. Communications are bad. Any surplus above subsistence needs in the western region, with the two towns of El Cayo and Benque Viejo in close proximity, is generally absorbed locally. The Agricultural Department has at times regarded the Indian settlers as anything but an economic asset, as their system is wasteful and encourages soil erosion.[1] Recently Mayan farm demonstrators have been trained with a view to improving methods. Cultivation is more settled in the north. Villages on private land are not so movable. The northern villages are laid out regularly in contrast to the higgledy-piggledy villages of the south. The Board of Agriculture's purchases come chiefly from its northern buying centres at Yo Creek, Orange Walk, August Pine Ridge, San Pablo and Louisville, and to a lesser degree from the south at Punta Gorda. Purchases in the west are negligible.

12,455 acres were estimated to produce 1000 lb. each at \$1.95 per 100 lb., less 20 per cent for costs (a figure which was intended to cover materials, seed, transport to market and a reduction for prices on farms). In general, material costs should

[1] 'The "milpa" system as practised from time immemorial by the Mayan Indians and adopted by other immigrants is outmoded as hopelessly uneconomic both from the point of view of the amount of labour required and the terrible waste of such natural assets as timber and soil fertility' (*Department of Agriculture Annual Report for 1948*).

be small, if not negligible. Seed costs only occur when no seed has been preserved from the previous season.

(*b*) *Rice*. Rice is grown chiefly in the rather swampy region behind Punta Gorda by East Indians and Caribs. Hill varieties are cultivated. The local seed has not been carefully bred (although the Rice Station at Punta Gorda is trying to remedy this[1]), so that the primitive form of reaping noted above has to be adopted. Cultivation has recently been extended to Monkey River and Barranco and small quantities for personal consumption are grown elsewhere. An experiment on a somewhat larger scale, planting between cohune palms, was made by Government in the middle of 1946, but was not a success. The very heavy rainfall in the south at harvest time prevents a real harvesting season. Large-scale reaping must be performed at one time if the labour force is to be retained and suitable periods cannot be expected. Reaping during heavy rains causes wastage. It would seem that rice cultivation must continue to be in the hands of the peasant farmer, who can more easily choose a reaping time for his small crop. The poor results of the government experiment were, however, partly due to inexperience and to lack of proper transport and storage facilities. Government maintains an efficient rice mill at Punta Gorda and a rather inefficient rice and corn mill at Belize. The percentage yield of rice from a given quantity of paddy, about 60 per cent., is much lower than that of Nigerian mills and may be due to poorer quality grain.

2461 acres were estimated to yield 1500 lb. of paddy each, at $2.90 per 100 lb. (compare the Nigerian price of 99 c. per 100 lb.), less 20 per cent for costs. Some of this is home-milled. The farmer has to thrash and dry paddy before sale, usually hiring government thrashers. Seed expenses are probably higher than with other crops. The production is only a small part of the Colony's consumption of what is a staple food of the creole population.

[1] 'Some progress was made towards the production of a pure seed supply to replace the present mixture of varieties which is normally sown' (*Department of Agriculture Annual Report for 1948*).

(*c*) *Beans and peas.* These, chiefly Red Kidney Beans and Black Beans, with smaller crops of Baby Red Beans and Congo Peas are grown throughout the Colony, chiefly by the Mayan Indians, whence the greater part of the marketed crop comes. Together with rice they form the staple food of the Belize population. Production meets only a small part of the Colony's consumption.

1600 acres were estimated to yield 300 lb. each at $7.00 per 100 lb., less 20 per cent for expenses, transport, etc.

(*d*) *Ground provisions and root crops.* These, comprising cassava, cocos, sweet potatoes and yams, are grown chiefly by the Caribs of Stann Creek and other coastal regions on smallholdings, often worked by women. There is domestic production of starch from cassava, some of which is retailed in the towns. A well-equipped starch factory at Canada Hill in the Stann Creek valley failed because the crop was insufficient to keep the factory going for more than a short period in the year. The price paid to farmers was too low to stimulate production of cassava. The product seems to have been of very good quality, but the enterprise seems to have been over-capitalised and the process already out of date at the time it was introduced.

1931 acres were estimated to yield 4000 lb. each at 2½ c. per lb., less 20 per cent for costs. (Costs are high on a mainly subsistence crop owing to rotting and wastage.)

(*e*) *Vegetables.* There is only a small attempt to supply what is anyway a limited market for vegetables.[1] Belize is the main market and is many miles from suitable market-garden land. The price is as high as that of vegetables of excellent quality imported from the United States. It seems that in the last thirty years the Indians and Spanish-Indians of the north have concentrated more and more on maize at the expense of what was once a more varied agriculture. This may be partly due to the high rewards of forest work and partly

[1] 'The relatively heavy crops planted in 1946 resulted in over-production for the relatively small demand in Belize which is the principal market . . . the annually recurrent difficulty of over-production during a short season and almost complete shortage at other times' (*Department of Agriculture Annual Report for 1947*).

to improved communications and the cheap import of tinned foods.

288 acres were estimated to yield 150 lb. each at 8 c. per lb., less 30 per cent for costs. This is mainly a marketed crop and sold through middlemen.

(*f*) *Bananas*. This once flourishing industry was attacked by disease. It was situated in the Stann Creek valley and along other rivers of the south (which enabled easy transport to the sea), but bananas are grown throughout the Colony. Fresh planting on new land has continued as the disease has spread.[1] Government is experimenting with the disease-resistant Lacatan banana. It is unlikely to find a market in the United States, which is accustomed to the Gros Michel banana. It is hoped that a market for the new banana will be found in the United Kingdom, where the bananaless war-years will have broken traditional preferences.[2] A small export trade continues by means of small, fast motor-vessels which pick up bananas at various points along the coast and carry them to New Orleans and Florida.[3]

1710 acres were estimated to yield 150 bunches each at 30 c. per bunch, less 20 per cent for costs.

(*g*) *Plantains*. These are common throughout the Colony and meet mainly domestic needs as a 'vegetable'.

1677 acres were estimated to yield 75 bunches each at 20 c. per bunch, less 20 per cent for costs.

(*h*) *Grapefruit and tinned juice*. A flourishing grapefruit industry has been established in the Stann Creek valley. There is a considerable export of tinned grapefruit juice. The successful nature of this enterprise, with an export crop, established as it has been with Jamaican capital and without needing government aid (other than a subsidy in wartime, to keep the orchards in condition when there were no exports), coupled with the fact

[1] 'This crop remains merely a "catch crop" for the small planters. Only on the most favourable sites does it remain profitable for longer than two years because of . . . leaf spot disease' (*Department of Agriculture Annual Report for 1945*).

[2] See *Department of Agriculture Annual Report for 1948*.

[3] See *Department of Agriculture Annual Report for 1946*.

that it has growing prospects and does not share the 'problems' and fears which beset other parts of the economy, has led, perhaps, to its significance in the economy being over-estimated.

1174 acres were estimated to yield 100 cases each. It was convenient to group the juice-tinning industry with the production of grapefruit, as the estimates are based on income tax figures and cannot be shown separately, only one firm being involved. For this reason the calculations cannot be given.[1]

(*i*) *Oranges*. 417 acres were estimated to yield 4500 lb. each at 30 c. per 100 lb., less 30 per cent for costs. This, unlike grapefruit, is not a 'plantation' crop, although it is now being developed in conjunction with grapefruit in the Stann Creek valley.

(*j*) *Other citrus*. 101 acres were estimated to yield 4500 lb. each at 30 c. per 100 lb., less 30 per cent for costs.

(*k*) *Coconuts*. Coconuts are found extensively along the coast and on the cays of the reef. They are used for food, for cooking oil, and in the manufacture of soap. During the war British Honduras, alone of the Caribbean colonies, permitted the export of nuts to the United States. In the West Indies generally production was held for local fat needs. It is hard to say how the acreage was assessed. A number of proper *cocals* are maintained, but the greater part of the acreage is 'natural'. In a year of good prices it is worth while and possible to step up exports considerably. In other years what is not consumed in the Colony is wasted. In 1946 prices up to $180 per 1000 nuts were obtained during the short export season, only to fall to $30 shortly after. A percentage of nuts exported had to be reserved for the soap industry. These might include reject nuts. In fact, in 1946 the local market was short of nuts during the high price period. In many agricultural products price responds to supply. When the market is saturated, prices fall. With coconut exports supply responds to price, as a year's demand is concentrated into a short buying period in which the market in the United States is strongly 'bullish'.

[1] See also Note on the Devaluation of the British Honduras Dollar, p. 139.

The calculation proved rather difficult and was approached in two ways. 6554 acres were estimated to yield 3000 nuts each at $67.00 per 1000, less 75 per cent for costs and wastage. The value of exports in the short season was estimated to equal the value of domestic consumption for the year. This might not be so in other years when exports might not be stimulated by such a good price.

It is tempting to speculate on the possibility of basing manufacturing industries on comparatively unused resources such as this. Apart, however, from the smallness of the local market (and the real smallness of the local supply), the resources are scattered over a large area. Only high prices will cause them to be brought to market in appreciable quantities. Once purses have been filled in a subsistence-minded population, with plenty of other things to turn its hand to, the supply becomes spasmodic and erratic, which is of no use to a manufacturing concern requiring a steady flow of materials. Attempts to tin lobsters some years ago failed for the same reason. Supplies were brought in to the cannery as the fishermen felt inclined and a steady flow of production could not be maintained. The grapefruit-juice tinning industry has none of these disadvantages as the area of supply is concentrated, the grapefruit holdings comparatively large and the farmers producing for the industry. Grapefruit is a 'plantation' crop rather than a peasant crop. So the supply is regular. If buying of a crop can be organised at many points throughout the Colony and the produce transported cheaply to a central point, this difficulty can be overcome. No industry can expect a steady supply to be *brought* to it, no matter what prices it offers. Lack of transport facilities has limited the growth of a large middleman class in agriculture. Transporters tend to be middlemen, but it is not their prime interest. This is the problem of the familiar triangle: agriculture; transport; industry. Other things being equal (i.e. costs and markets), if you have two of the three the other one will be made. If you have only one the other two will not be made. This is what the dreamer who looks at underdeveloped colonies and imagines gigantic possibilities always overlooks.[1] A transport system as a whole is one of the assets of a Colony, whatever hands it is in. But it cannot exist *in vacuo.* Neither can either of the other constituents, except that agriculture can exist on its markets, first near markets, later farther ones as a rudimentary transport system develops. The first thing then (in an agricultural community) is to enlarge markets for agriculture and gradually increase the assets 'agriculture' and 'transport' until they are big enough to carry the third, 'manufacture'. In a Colony with rich mines, of course, the problem does not exist in the same terms.

(*l*) *Pineapples.* 297 acres were estimated to yield 150 pineapples at 10 c. each, less 20 per cent for costs.

Horses and mules. The estimated increase in stocks per annum was about the same as the value of the imports. The local stock was therefore assumed to be static, deaths equalling births, and no figure was entered.[2]

(*m*) *Cattle.* Cattle are reared mainly along the Belize River, in the Cayo–Benque Viejo region to the west, and, less, in the north around Corozal and Orange Walk. There is a small consumption of fresh milk, but it has not yet reached a significant point.[3] Some butter is made, at a higher price than imported butter.

The stock of 16,000 was estimated to consist of 14,000 females and 2000 males. 10,500 young were estimated to have been produced. The natural mortality was put at 10 per cent or 1600, and losses from drought (an annual feature) [4] and other

[1] Mr Adolph Woermann, the grandson of the man who signed the first treaty with the natives which gave the Cameroons to Germany, described to me many years ago the potentialities of South-West Africa; how if you had a large population there you could install great irrigation works and turn the desert to fruitful land, and how if you had great irrigation works you could bring in a large population, but that neither was practicable unless they could be magically produced simultaneously.

[2] 'Horses are quite numerous but of a small saddle type and are not used as farm animals to do farm labour' (*Department of Agriculture Annual Report for 1947*).

[3] See *Department of Agriculture Annual Report for 1945*.

[4] 'Cattle are kept almost entirely on the ranching system, although many of the ranches are but small in size. The limiting factor to the number of cattle that can be kept is the amount of grazing available in the dry season' (*Department of Agriculture Annual Report for 1944*).

causes at 1400. The annual increase in numbers was estimated at 1500. Slaughterings were estimated at 6000, at $28.00 each (average weight 400 lb. at 7 c. per lb.). The increase in numbers was valued at the same rate. Costs were estimated at 25 per cent.

(*n*) *Sheep and goats.* The stock of 1700 was estimated to contain 850 females, producing 1275 young. Slaughterings were estimated at 600, deaths at 200, increase in numbers at 400. The value was taken as $2.50 a pair. Costs were estimated at 20 per cent, which is probably high.

(*o*) *Pigs.* Pigs play a large part in subsistence agriculture, as the number of Indian villages called San Antonio bears tribute. A considerable quantity reaches the market, and pork is the commonest meat.[1] In the north 'hog lard' is produced, and in Stann Creek some pork is salted.

The stock of 11,000 was estimated to contain 5500 sows, producing 22,000 young a year. Deaths were estimated at 1500, the annual increase in numbers at 500 and the slaughterings at 20,000. The value was reckoned at $6.50 each (average weight 50 lb. at 13 c. per lb.). Costs were estimated, probably highly, at 20 per cent.

(*p*) *Poultry.* The stock of 68,000 was estimated to contain 57,500 hens, producing 50 eggs each. The annual increase in numbers was estimated at 6000, the sales of fowls at 30,000 and the consumption of eggs at 2,750,000. Costs were estimated at 25 per cent.

(*q*) *Alligator skins.* These are included here as they are probably obtained by agriculturists. The estimate closely follows the export figure.

(*r*) *Cohune.* The cohune palm is ubiquitous, associated with

[1] 'The keeping of pigs is widespread throughout the Colony and it is interesting to find that, even on some of the Cays, where there is little opportunity for breeding, almost every householder buys one or two store pigs each year for fattening on the household and garden refuse. . . . The number of pigs over any period varies with the amount of food available. In the north this food is maize, in the south it is rejected bananas' (*Department of Agriculture Annual Report for 1945*). There is thus an element of double-counting here as the maize or bananas consumed by the pigs also appear to some extent under those items. This does not occur with cattle, as they are 'ranched', i.e. depend on the natural vegetation.

the more fertile soils, and is really a forest tree. The kernel has an extremely high percentage of oil, but the nut is exceptionally hard to crack. A company was started to exploit the nut near Punta Gorda, but failed, owing to the usual over-capitalisation, the royalty on the nut-cracking machines and the dispersed nature of the crop. This last meant that to achieve adequate supplies a large area had to be covered. As the nuts were bought in the shell, the return that could be offered per lb. was small.[1] During 1946 a small export was made by the Import Control Office, buying cracked nuts. These nuts were cracked by hand, using a kind of hammer and anvil. Thus instead of bringing the whole nuts to the cracking machine, the machine was taken to the nuts. Even so there is considerable breakage of kernels in cracking, as great force has to be applied.

(*s*) *Sugar*. The sugar crop is grown mainly in the north around Corozal and to a lesser extent in the south around Punta Gorda. The northern crop is sold to the Corozal Sugar Factory (apart from that consumed on the farm or used in rum-making). This meets the whole of the Colony's sugar needs in a normal year and can be milled in four months. Cane is ratooned for anything up to fifteen years. The crop is mainly grown on large holdings with employed labour.

1752 acres were estimated to yield 15 tons each, at $5.50 per ton, less 50 c. for transport and 25 per cent for expenses. This gave a value for output of $98,550. It was possible to apply a light check from the income side, using the Census:

248 labourers	@ $300	$74,400
4 teamsters	@ $300	1,200
4 others	@ $300	1,200
14 foremen	@ $500	7,000
4 farmers (from Income Tax)	@ $2000	8,000
		$91,800

[1] 'It is regretted that the [cohune nut] industry which at first showed signs of becoming a thriving one came to a standstill in the early portion of the year. . . . Sporadic nut gathering has continued however on a small scale' (*Annual Report of the Labour Department for the year ended 31st December 1945*).

The high earnings given for labour were estimated to make good the larger labour force employed in the season. The final result was taken as $96,000.

(*t*) *Other crops*. It was impossible to estimate the value of the common, but occasional, growth of mangoes, avocado pears, pawpaws, melons, cocoa, coffee, breadfruit, eggplant, custard apples, star apples, etc., although the total production would be far from negligible. Mangoes in season, for example, appear to be an important food item, and it seems that sales of other produce (including meat) fall off during the mango season. A figure of $50,000 has been inserted to cover these items.

2. MINING AND QUARRYING

Mining is the thing on which most prosperous colonies chiefly depend. It alone, in these days, attracts the kind of foreign capital which results in real investment and development. Roads and railways spring up in its wake, markets are provided and agriculture can develop with at least the assurance of this market to give it stability. Otherwise it can look for stability only at the subsistence level, in feeding the mouths of those who grow food. Agriculture can rarely attract much capital naturally unless labour costs are so low relative to world prices for products that good profits can be expected,[1] and forest industries only enough to ensure the extraction of natural capital which is relatively cheaply got. Mining encourages concentrated settlements and the acquisition of industrial skills. Near them something other than craft industries may be born and flourish. The taxation of mines provides surpluses over and above the bare costs of administration, which can be used for further development, for investment in transport systems, roads, canals and railways, airports, to open up other areas, and for improving the welfare of the whole community in whose area the mines are situated. The colonies of today can, with a few

[1] The investment of Europeans in agriculture in South, Central and East Africa was based on cheap labour, and even so the margin of profit was not great. The large tracts of land set aside in Northern Rhodesia by the British South Africa Co. and North Charterland Company were only to a very small extent taken up.

freak exceptions, be divided into the relatively prosperous ones with prospects and the sick ones without, simply on this basis of whether they have mines or not. The spectacle of South Africa, with its agriculture and manufactures built up on the prosperity of its gold mines, and of Northern Rhodesia, converted in twenty-five years from a grant-aided colony to a relatively prosperous one, illustrate this. Yet neither of these two countries can show anything like the same spread of educational and medical services over its population as can British Honduras. This is significant when it is recorded that there are no mines in the Colony. Whether there is any, as yet hidden, mineral wealth is unknown. Although stories of traces of gold and oil recur, there is little of even circumstantial evidence to support them. The unexplored condition of a great part of the country makes it impossible to say what the future may hold, but whatever it may be, it has no significance for the economy of today.

Two government quarries are operated, one in the Belize district and one, more spasmodically, in the Toledo district. Their output is used for road-metalling. Stone is taken in other places, including some heavy stone from the sea by fishermen and boatmen. The Census gives seven quarrymen in one table and twelve in another. Averaging the two a figure of $3000 has been inserted. In theory stone is bought at cost by the various works undertaken. The error may be anything up to 100 per cent.

3. FISHING

Fishing occurs along the whole length of the coast, especially among the Caribs. Fish is a most important food south of Belize. There has been some export of fresh lobsters to the United States (and other places by aeroplane), most of which appears to have escaped the Customs records. The presence of quantities of Guatemalan quetzals and United States dollars in circulation in Punta Gorda suggests a further unmeasured export of fish to Guatemala, probably by British Honduras Caribs to Carib settlements in Guatemala.

It was possible to calculate the output of fishing in two ways. Using the Census figures the income of fishing was reckoned:[1]

3 employers	@ $500 .	$1,500
303 own-account workers	@ $300 .	90,900
17 employees	@ $200 .	3,400
281 subsidiary fishermen	@ $50 .	14,050
		$109,850

To check this the Collector of Customs' returns of fish sold in markets in 1948 were used, on the assumption that there was little change from 1946. Not all fish, however, is sold in markets. It was estimated that 25 per cent of fish in the Belize district was, and 50 per cent in Stann Creek is sold directly from boats or consumed by fishermen and their families, but that all at Corozal is sold in the market, which is at the end of the pier. Adjustments were made to provide for this. Punta Gorda, not being included, was reckoned on a population basis, having similar characteristics to the town of Stann Creek, and as having a catch of two-fifths that of Stann Creek. Again on the basis of population two-thirds of the Stann Creek catch was added for other fishing villages along the coast. Exports were added and a further figure for unrecorded exports, based on an address by Mr Dawson to the Fisheries Conference at Miami at the end of 1948, when he gave the export of lobsters for 1946.[2] No account was taken of conchs. It is not known how much they are used for food, or their shells for other purposes. These calculations resulted in the table on p. 69.

This includes turtles. It is close to the income calculation but probably underestimates output north of Belize and ex-

[1] 'There has been little change in the numbers engaged in fishing since the Census of 1901.' In times of distress the number seems to increase. '1931 showed an enlarged number, this being attributed to numbers of people then engaged in fishing for purposes of subsistence and for lack of opportunity in other occupations' (*Census of British Honduras, 1946*, chap. VII, para. 17). This demonstrates the adaptability of the people and the tendency to turn from one occupation to another.

[2] This is an example of information received quite fortuitously on a file which was passed to me in another connection.

Output of Fishing

Corozal	$3,642
Stann Creek	18,484
Belize	23,564
Punta Gorda	7,393
Other coastal villages	12,000
Exports:	
dried fish	4,958
fresh fish	4,836
tortoise shell	592
lobsters	31,607
	$107,076

cludes exports in the south. It has been rounded up to $110,000. The margin of error is likely to be small.

Hunting. The Census gives five persons employed in hunting. It was impossible to value their output or the output of hunting. The value of alligator skins has been included under Agriculture. The value of venison, gibnut and armadillo consumed has been treated as negligible for the purposes of this study. It is, in any case, doubtful if anyone is primarily a hunter, and hunting is probably a subsidiary 'industry'. Indeed in British Honduras a 'hunter' is popularly one who seeks for mahogany trees rather than game, and this may have caused an error in the Census. No figure was entered.

4. FORESTRY

It proved possible to divide Forestry into four components: Timber-getting, Firewood, Chicle-bleeding and Forest cultivation, based on the Census. Many firms engaged in Timber-getting are sawmillers as well, especially in the pine industry, where the production is of sawn wood. It was difficult to separate one side of their activities from the other. Sawmilling was therefore included in Timber-getting rather than separately under secondary industries. The dressing of timbers is, perhaps, more suitably classed as a primary industry.

The greater part of the easily accessible forest land in the

Colony has already been worked out.[1] It will in time recover (the time factor being about a century) if cutting is successfully controlled in the meantime. Cutting of immature trees will, of course, delay regeneration in the north, where mahogany is indigenous, and would eradicate it in the south. The extraction of mahogany and cedar, with some subsidiary hardwoods,[2] now takes place chiefly along the Guatemalan and Mexican borders, and (until the closing of the Guatemalan frontier in 1947) over them. Mahogany trees occur in isolation in the forest and 'hunters' are employed to locate them. When this has been done a truck-pass, or rough road, is cut to them, with side traces to individual trees. The trees are cut, hauled to the truck-pass and carried by camions to the nearest river. Even with the development of motor transport the areas available to small contractors operating for foreign firms with their capital is limited. The firms generally advance cash, plant and stores to contractors, who in turn advance cash to the workers and then go out to find and cut the timber on a particular concession. The timber cut is measured by the firm's licensed measurer, whose figures have been accepted both by the contractor and (until very recently) by the Customs Department. One firm works its own land and has installed a railway from the headwaters of the New River at Hillbank Lagoon to the western border at Gallon Jug, where there is a permanent camp. Other camps are seasonal and the workers come from Belize. Logs are floated down the Belize River when it floods. The New River is too sluggish and logs are towed north to Corozal and thence round by sea to the sawmill and ships at Belize.

There has been increased exploitation of the pine forests in recent years, with exports of house timbers to Jamaica.[3] Pine, unlike mahogany, is concentrated and occurs in areas of poor soil. The small and fairly movable circular sawmill is used and the wood is sawn at the spot where it is cut.

[1] 'The 1946 numbers, although considerably higher than in 1931, show little increase over the early years of the century' (*Census of British Honduras, 1946*, chap. VII, para. 14).

[2] Santa Maria, Yemeri and Banak.

[3] See Table VI.

The chicle industry uses, mainly, the labour of Mayan Indians and Spanish-Indians who bleed the sapodilla tree for the gum from which chewing-gum is made. The best quality chicle is found in the north. In the south the quality is poorer and it is known as Crown gum. The two are usually mixed to some extent before export. It has already been noted that the *chiclero* is also a *milpero* and that chicle-bleeding competes with agriculture for his labour, to the disadvantage of agriculture.

A certain amount of forest regeneration and planting is undertaken by the Forest Department.

(*a*) *Timber-getting and sawmilling.* Some rather different estimates for the labour force were found, ranging from 1030 in the Labour Report to 1374 in the Census. This may be due to differences in definition. The Labour Officer in his 'Notes on the Census' gave different figures for average earnings from those in his Report. The income tax profits for fifteen concerns and individuals, including sawmills and timber-contractors, were available. In the Forestry Report the whole industry is admirably detailed under production and export. The part of the industry which was carried on in Guatemala and Mexico was included. It was assumed that the number of workers employed in Timber-getting over the Colony's borders bore the same proportion to those inside the Colony as re-exports of timber bore to domestic exports. This is likely to be on the low side compared with other years, as re-exports were exceptionally low in 1946. The rates of pay given in the Labour Report were then worked out for the season and averaged, proving, at $313, to be much lower than the estimates in the Labour Officer's Notes. The total internal wage was then calculated and the total external wage on an average of $303, as the imports from Guatemala and Mexico were mahogany and cedar, the rates for workers in these woods being lower than the average. The earnings of tractor- and truck-drivers were then calculated from the Labour Report.

For the sawmills the numbers employed as given in the Labour Report and in the Census for the Belize district tallied closely, the difference being accounted for by salary-earners.

They both probably covered the same ground. The Census gave a further 112 in other districts. This was accepted. There were also 17 supervisors and clerks and 166 machinery attendants and operators. These calculations gave the following earnings from sawmilling:

Supervisors and clerks	\$21,828
Machinery attendants and operators .	116,200
Labourers @ \$420	106,260
Labourers in districts @ \$350 . .	39,200
	\$283,488

Use was again made of employers' returns of wages. No evidence was available for salaries, and a notional figure was entered. To arrive at the materials used by the timber industry the Customs import figures were examined for free imports of machinery, plant etc. Beside these are duty-paid imports and imports on which the duty was refunded. It was estimated that the value of timber consumed locally was \$200,000. This may be a low figure. No account was taken of the consumption of timber by the industry itself. These calculations enabled a rough account of Timber-getting and Sawmilling to be drawn up:

Account for Timber-getting and Sawmilling

	\$000		\$000
		Wages—labour—timber:	
Gross exports . .	2181	internal . . .	429
Local consumption .	200	external . . .	79
		sawmill . . .	284
		Tractor-drivers, etc.:	
		internal . . .	142
		external . . .	28
		Foremen . . .	61
		Salary-earners . .	41
		Profits: companies .	343
		contractors .	31
		Royalty . . .	150
		Other expenses (free imports= \$348,000) .	793
	2381		2381

From the account the net output, after deducting the profits not due to resident factors of production, was:

	$000
Wages	1023
Salaries	41
Profits	39
Royalty	150
	1253

(*b*) *Firewood.* The Census gave 79 employed, of whom 68 were own-account workers, one an unpaid helper and 10 employees. Own-account workers were estimated to earn $400, employees $300, to give $30,200. The Forestry Report gave the value of the output of firewood and charcoal at $31,456. The latter figure was accepted.

(*c*) *Chicle-bleeding.* The Labour Officer's Notes estimated 1600 *chicleros* at less than $500 per annum and 80 muleteers at $250 per annum. The Income Tax Department assessed 16 persons in the chicle industry, including *chicleros* at $79,736. The Labour Report gave 1788 *chicleros* and 93 muleteers, for a ten-month season at (for *chicleros*) $125 per month. Chicle earnings vary enormously, as is evident from the income tax returns (some contractors returning payments to *chicleros*). The range is from $200 to $3000. Export of chicle was about two-thirds domestic and one-third re-export.[1] The assumption has been made that *chicleros* were paid and spent their money inside the Colony, even though working across the border. From the Forest Department's chicle licences an average price of 60 c. per lb. was taken. The muleteers' incomes were estimated at $250 per annum, the profits of dealers at $16,000, to give a net output for Chicle-bleeding of:

		$000	
Earnings—	*chicleros*	961	(approx. 1747 earning $500)
	muleteers	23	
Profits—	others	16	
		1000	

[1] See Table VII.

(*d*) *Forest Cultivation.* The Census gives 32 persons employed in Forest Cultivation. The output has been estimated at $16,400. The margin of error is large.

5. MANUFACTURING AND REPAIR

Apart from the government electricity and ice plant, the sugar factory, some boat-building and repair yards and very small factories for aerated waters, rum, soap and cigarettes, this group consists of small craftsmen making clothes, furniture, etc., and repair men of all kinds.[1]

From this point onwards in the Output Table cross-checks were rarely available and the output has been calculated on incomes, based on the Census figures of the numbers employed, and on profits. The labour force of the small industries, most of which will require some skill, will probably be constant throughout the year, as will the numbers of craftsmen working. The estimates of incomes of different occupations can be derived with some accuracy from income tax returns and employers' returns of wages paid. As the calculations mostly follow the same pattern, the details will not be given unless some other method is adopted, or cross-checks are available.

(*a*) *Food:* (i) *Slaughtering and meat products.* 11 butchers and 5 employees, $6750. This figure does not include butchers employed under other industry-groupings. 34 butchers appear under Commerce.

(ii) *Grain-milling, cereal products.* 5 workers, $2300. This may be an underestimate.

(iii) *Bread, cakes and biscuits.* 91 bakers and 66 employees and apprentices, $59,050. The earnings of female own-account workers were estimated to be lower than those of males.

(iv) *Sugar-milling.* The Agricultural Report gives production at the Corozal factory as 808 tons of sugar from 8962 tons of

[1] 'That the factories and workshops are for the most part very small is clear from the fact that 945 persons (out of 2551) were on their "own account". 71 persons were described as employers. This is more than the total of owners and managers and indicates that many of the employers were themselves working tradesmen' (*Census of British Honduras, 1946*, chap. VII, para. 22).

cane. The production is of 'plantation white' and brown sugar. The Colony normally consumes some 1400 to 1600 tons of sugar, which is largely met by the factory.[1] There is a 'concealed' import of sugar in sweetened condensed milk, which is widely used. There were two small brown-sugar factories in the Toledo district, for which the Census gives three employees. This secondary industry is an exception in that it is seasonal (three to five months each year) and draws a varying labour force. Estimating the value of the gross output at $105 per ton (approximately the average import price), the following account can be drawn up:

Account for Sugar-milling

	$000		$000
Sugar produced	90,000	Sugar cane	49,291
		Wages and salaries	22,500
		Profits	12,384
		Expenses	5,825
	90,000		90,000

This gives a net output of $34,884.

(v) *Confectionery and other food products.* 3 employers, 11 workers, $5000.

The combined Food Output Table is:

	$000
Slaughtering and meat products	7
Grain-milling, cereal products	2
Bread, cakes and biscuits	59
Sugar-milling	35
Confectionery and other food products	5
	108

(*b*) *Beverages:* (i) *Brewing and distilling.* The distilling of rum is subsidiary to sugar-planting and sugar-milling. A number of sugar plantations (varying around half a dozen) have small stills. In 1946 all these were in the north, in the vicinity of Corozal. There was an unknown amount of illicit home-distilling in the south. The total rum produced, according to the Customs Report, was 25,345·168 proof gallons, or, 16,928

[1] See Table VIII.

liquid gallons, which was lower than usual.[1] It is generally sold by producers at $1.25 per proof gallon. An arbitrary one-third has been deducted for expenses of manufacture, other than wages, giving a net output of $21,121.

(ii) *Fruit juices, cordials and aerated waters.* This excludes the output of the grapefruit juice tinning industry. The Census gives 73 engaged, including 3 employers, 4 unemployed and 1 own-account worker. The Labour Officer gives 57 employees under aerated waters. Five employers were assessed to tax.

Profits	$26,590
Wages est.	19,500
	$46,090

(iii) *Ice-making.* The Census gives 4 employees. There is a government ice plant in Belize, run in conjunction with the electricity plant, with which its accounts are inextricably mixed up. It is believed that if it was separately accounted for and fully charged for electric current it would show a loss. As it is, any such loss is a deduction from electricity profits, shown below. A figure of $1200 has been inserted for employees. There were no other ice plants in 1946, but there is now a small one at Benque Viejo. No private concern could profitably compete in Belize with the government ice plant.

The combined Beverages Output Table is:

	$000
Distilling	21
Fruit juices, cordials and aerated waters	46
Ice	1
	68

(*c*) *Tobacco.* The Customs Report yields some information on the tobacco manufacturing industry.[2] The income tax returns are useful, and on these bases the net output of the industry has been estimated at $40,000. No account has been taken of locally grown and cured tobacco, only a negligible amount having entered into the manufacture of cigarettes and tobacco.[3]

[1] See Table IX. [2] See Table X. [3] *Customs Report, 1946*, para. 25.

(*d*) *Oils and fats.* 17 own-account workers.

(*e*) *Chemicals.* This embraces the soap factory. The net output is estimated, in the usual way, at $16,325.

(*f*) *Wood and cork* (other than sawmilling). This covers 58 cabinet-makers, 52 employees and 17 apprentices.

(*g*) *Paper, printing and photography:* (i) *Printing and bookbinding.* This includes earnings of employees in the Government Printing Office. It covers 6 printers and 59 employees, $43,271.

(ii) *Photography.* 10 photographers and 4 employees, $8100.

(*h*) *Leather* (tanning and leather goods, not footwear). 3 own-account workers and 6 employees.

(*i*) *Apparel, textile articles:* (i) *Tailoring.* 144 tailors, 47 employees and 11 apprentices, $91,400.

(ii) *Dressmaking.* 309 dressmakers and 37 employees, $85,075.

(iii) *Garment-making, embroidery.* 13 workers, $3200.

(iv) *Hats, bags, hosiery and knitted goods.* 16 workers, $3200.

(v) *Footwear.* 112 shoemakers, 61 employees and 18 apprentices, $92,669.

(vi) *Other made-up textile articles.* 10 workers, $3000.

The combined table for Apparel and Textile Articles Output is:

	$000
Tailoring	91
Dressmaking	85
Garment-making, embroidery	3
Hats, bags, hosiery, knitted goods	3
Footwear	93
Other made-up textile articles	3
	278

(*j*) *Electricity and water:* (i) *Electricity.* This includes the surplus of the government plant in Belize and the municipal plant in Corozal, together with 34 employees, $68,204.

(ii) *Water.* 5 employees, $2000.

These are men engaged in fetching water from up the Belize River during the dry season, March-May, when Belize, which is dependent on rain water, runs short. It is probably an overestimate, as the Census was taken in the dry season, but water is to some extent fetched, in some years, for the greater part of the year.

(*k*) *Non-metallic minerals.* 2 workers.

(*l*) *Metal manufacture:* (i) *Blacksmithing.* 7 workers, $4100.

(ii) *Tinsmithing.* 15 workers, $9300.

(iii) *Other metal.* 16 workers, $9800.

(*m*) *Machinery and vehicles:* (i) *Electrical machinery.* 6 workers, $2100.

(ii) *Boats.* There are some half-dozen boat-building and repair yards at Belize and the cays. The boats constructed are usually small sailing boats, either pleasure craft or, more usually, boats for carrying freight up and down the coast, and motor launches, with an occasional motor vessel of up to about 50 tons. 44 boat-builders and shipwrights, 124 employees and apprentices were estimated to earn $104,400.

(iii) *Motor vehicles and bicycles.* This is a repair industry. 21 employers, 61 own-account workers, 100 employees and 25 apprentices were estimated to earn $117,300. The margin of error may be as much as 25 per cent.

(iv) *Motor vehicle bodies.* 3 employees, $1200.

(v) *Other vehicles.* 5 employees, $1500.

(vi) *Machinery.* 22 workers, $10,600.

The combined table for the output of Machinery and Vehicles is:

	$000
Electrical machinery	2
Boats	104
Motor vehicles and bicycles	117
Motor vehicle bodies	1
Other vehicles	1
Machinery	10
	235

(*n*) *Instruments, jewellery and other:* (i) *Watchmaking and jewellery.* 17 watchmakers and 2 employees, $14,000.

(ii) *Other.* 9 workers, $3900.

(In parenthesis it may be added that the construction of these tables suggests that the classifications of the West Indian Census, however applicable to Jamaica, hardly seem appropriate for British Honduras.)

6. CONSTRUCTION

The same methods have been used to arrive at the net output of Construction.

(*a*) *Building*. Nearly all buildings are made of wood. There is no building stone near Belize, and Belize sets the pattern for the whole country. This accounts for there being 354 carpenters among a total employed in Building Construction of 536.[1] A few larger, hurricane-proof buildings have been built in concrete. The pole-and-thatch, plastered houses common in the districts and outskirts of the small towns are 'home-made'.

(*b*) *Road*. Road building is exceptionally costly. The soil is not suitable for the construction of earth roads. All roads have to be metalled, with the metalling often brought long distances. Most of them are tarred as well. The depreciation of roads through swampy lands is rapid and maintenance costs are high.

(*c*) *Other construction*. 1 employer, 2 own-account workers and 10 employees.

7. TRANSPORT AND COMMUNICATIONS

(*a*) *Rail*. It has already been noted that this covers only two employees on a logging railway of a timber concern.

(*b*) *Motor*. Motor transport is as yet not very developed, and is mainly an offshoot of other businesses or in the hands of individuals. In 1946 there were only four roads of any length. The oldest, from Belize to Orange Walk and Corozal covers mainly low-lying marshland and pine forest as far as Orange Walk. From there it goes through the richer land between the New and Hondo Rivers, but duplicates the water transport of the rivers and sea. It was extended to the Mexican border, but

[1] 'Evidence of the small scale of much of the building is that 138 persons were working on their own account employing no paid labour, while only 4 were described as employers' (*Census of British Honduras, 1946*, chap. VII, para. 26).

connections on the other side were not complete. The Mexican provinces of Quintana Roo and Yucatan have poor connections with the rest of Mexico and the value of this road may increase with time. At the present the entrepôt trade of Belize with Mexico goes by sea. The road to El Cayo in the west had not been completed. It has since opened up a fertile area with agricultural potentialities and has killed the Belize River traffic. A road up the Stann Creek valley for 25 miles connected the citrus lands and grapefruit juice tinning industry with the only deep-water port in the Colony. A road from Punta Gorda to San Antonio brought the rice of the East Indians and the surplus products of the Mayan Indians to market. Passenger traffic is still largely by lorry, taxi or private cars, which were few in 1946. Most heavy goods from the north still went to Belize by sea. The timber industry hardly uses the roads at all.

Only one employer was wholly engaged in motor transport. There were 41 own-account taxi- and truck-drivers, whose incomes were derived from income tax assessments, and 128 employees of different kinds.

(*c*) *Other road transport*. This covers transport by pack mules on forest trails and the draymen of the towns. There is no long-distance carriage of goods by road other than by motor transport. The drays, which are light, two-wheeled carts, ply for hire in the towns.

There were 49 working on their own account and 26 employees.

(*d*) *Water*. This is still the chief means of transporting freight and (to the south) passengers. The Colony has been settled from the sea, along the coast and up the rivers. As a result the waterways connect up the main areas of settlement, the New River, the Rio Hondo and the Sarstoon River, and water transport can still hold its own with road transport. Only the Belize River transport, which was long and difficult, with hauls over rapids and runs, has given way. Locally-owned motor vessels ply to Chetumal in Mexico, Puerto Cortes in Spanish Honduras and further afield to the United States. The larger vessels calling at British Honduras are foreign-owned. Motor vessels of up to 50 tons carry freight and passengers up and down the coast. Small sailing vessels and even dugouts carry produce between points on the coast and to market, in the shelter of the barrier reef.

The Census gives 5 employers and owners, 3 pilots, 18 captains and others working on their own account, and 520 employees of various kinds, including stevedores.

(*e*) *Air*. All air transport is foreign-owned, either Central American or, to a much smaller degree, British. The majority of passengers to and from other countries arrive at and leave the Colony by air. There are connections to all Central American capitals, New Orleans, Florida and Jamaica.

(*f*) *Communications*. This class includes the surpluses of the Post Office, which maintains the postal services and radio telegraph communications with Jamaica and other countries and Punta Gorda, and of the Telephones Department, which maintains internal telephone and telegraph services to almost all settlements as far south as Monkey River, and an extension to Chetumal in Mexico. There were 78 employees.

The consideration of communications suggests, if the Stann Creek valley road were extended a short distance to connect with the Belize–Cayo road, that Stann Creek, with its deeper water, would be a more natural centre for the Colony than Belize, which is backed by six miles of mangrove swamp and a further thirty-mile radius of swampy, barren land. As the main transport connections of Belize are by water, Stann Creek would be at no disadvantage, and a Stann Creek–Cayo road would meet the Belize–Cayo road at the point where it enters the most fertile part.[1] It might be wiser to plan future road programmes with such a development in mind. The heavy road-maintenance charges in an under-developed Colony suggest that the north should continue to depend on water transport,

[1] 'The "feeder road" for the Stann Creek Valley is that from Middlesex to Roaring Creek. The building of this road should enable the products of the livestock industry of the Cayo District to reach the Stann Creek Valley at economic rates' (*Department of Agriculture Annual Report, 1948*). Since this was written the building of this road has begun as part of the 'compensation' for the devaluation of the British Honduras dollar and as relief work.

with which it is well provided, with only feeder roads to the rivers. Roads to the south from the Stann Creek valley would open up new areas with potentialities. At present the major road scheme is for feeder roads connecting the various settlements now on the rivers with the main roads. In the north this means going to considerable expense, which will recur in maintenance, to duplicate an existing transport system. The extinction of water transport on the Belize River makes them necessary there. In the south they are being well used to connect subsistence communities with markets and so to stimulate production beyond the bare needs of subsistence.

8. COMMERCE

(*a*) *Retail and wholesale trade.* This figure includes the assessed profits of 187 businesses at $626,129 and the profits and earnings of 270 owners and managers not assessed to tax, with 4 fishermen, 34 butchers, 248 hawkers, etc., and 1092 employees of various kinds.

(*b*) *Finance:* (i) *Banking and finance.* This covers the profits of banks and moneylenders, less profits not due to resident factors of production, and the earnings of employees. The bank is foreign-owned. The value of its services was taken to be the earnings of its employees. The problem of bank profits, which arise from interest charged on loans and interest from investments less the cost of services charged or given free to lenders, does not arise, as the profits are not due to resident factors of production and do not concern this study. For that reason the amount of maintenance and depreciation of bank property, which is normally included when profits are excluded, is also excluded, as it is a charge against foreign profits. The moneylenders included are petty one-man concerns dealing in small loans. Their profits are considered to be the value of their services. The estimated net output was $34,445.

(ii) *Insurance.* There are no local insurance companies. The figure of $1000 was inserted, based on income tax returns, to cover the services of local agents.

(iii) *Accountancy and book-keeping.* Profits and wages were estimated at $40,000.

(iv) *Real estate management.* Earnings were estimated at $10,800.

(v) *Other mixed agencies.* 4 employers, 7 own-account workers and 17 employees were estimated to earn $25,200.

The combined table for the net output of Finance is:

	$000
Banking and finance	34
Insurance	1
Accountancy and book-keeping	40
Real estate management	11
Other mixed agencies	25
	111

9. RECREATIONAL SERVICE

(*a*) *Cinemas.* Profits and earnings of employees, $35,142.

(*b*) *Other.* It was not possible to dissect this rather general classification. 38 employees were estimated to earn $11,400.

10. PROFESSIONAL SERVICE

(*a*) *Medical and hygiene.* This includes earnings of employees in the government medical and health services, professional profits and other employees' earnings.

(*b*) *Undertaking, cemetery and other hygienic services.* 28 workers estimated to earn $8400.

(*c*) *Education.* The educational system is run by the churches with the assistance of government grants, except for two small government schools taken over from one mission. Elementary education is compulsory throughout the country. The figure includes 419 employed and independent teachers.

(*d*) *Religion.* The churches' returns of salaries paid were averaged to arrive at the earnings of clergymen, missionaries and other religious workers. This was $727. This does not include unpaid services, which account for a large part of the staff of the Roman Catholic Church. The average was applied to 101 religious workers (not including labourers, etc.) to yield $73,427.

11. PUBLIC SERVICE

(*a*) *Armed Forces.* There were 611 officers and other ranks in the Armed Forces stationed in the Colony. These were mainly the British Honduras Battalion of the North Caribbean Force. The battalion was disbanded in 1947, but in 1948, as a result of threats from Guatemala, a contingent of British troops was stationed in the Colony. There seems, therefore, every likelihood of there being armed forces for some time to come. It is, however, disputable whether British forces should be included in the national income, as they will be included in that of the United Kingdom. The case of the British Honduras Battalion was different as, although paid for by United Kingdom funds, it consisted mainly of local men. It had a considerable effect on the economy, and on its disbandment the members had to be absorbed while the income which had maintained them ceased. The earnings have been taken at a rather low average to take account of discharges during the year.

(*b*) *Administration.* This covers government employees not classified elsewhere; foremen, tradesmen, boatmen, messengers, truck-drivers, engineers, inspectors, clerks and labourers. Some of these should probably come under the heading Construction.

(*c*) *Law.* 3 judges and magistrates, 6 lawyers and 17 clerks. A District Commissioner is a magistrate, and according to whether he considers his magisterial or his administrative duties more important he will come under this or the previous heading.

(*d*) *Police, prisons.* The earnings are taken from the Colony's Financial Statements.

12. PERSONAL SERVICE

(*a*) *Hotels, restaurants, cafés.* Earnings of 18 hotels, boarding-houses, restaurants and bars were assessed for income tax at $25,107. 123 not assessed were estimated to yield $61,500. Earnings of 65 cooks and domestic servants were estimated at $9282.

(*b*) *Laundry, dry cleaning.* This is a strange category as there are no laundries and the few self-styled dry cleaners are ineffective. The group contains 3 employers and 397 own-account workers and employees. These would seem to be either individuals who take in washing or persons who might equally well be classed as domestic servants. They have been included at a figure for average earnings of $117 per annum, which is the rate given by the Labour Officer in his Notes for domestic servants and includes rations. Washing clothes is the lowest-paid domestic service. The rate is, however, much lower than one would expect.

(*c*) *Hairdressing*. 46 own-account workers and 4 employees.

(*d*) *Domestic Service*. This includes chauffeurs, messengers, cooks, gardeners, housekeepers and 126 laundresses apart from domestic servants proper. The total is 1083. Unlike so many colonies, domestic servants are undoubtedly the lowest paid part of the population. 'Perks' and pickings no doubt supplement their meagre earnings to some extent.

13. ODD JOBS

The Census gives 1396 persons as in ill-defined industries. This is a large figure, and no doubt if adequate information were available the bulk of these could be distributed over other occupations. Of these, 1364 are labourers, the rest clerks and typists. They probably cover the more mobile (between jobs) part of the population and possibly a lot of temporary unemployment. A figure had, however, to be given for them and they have been estimated at $220 each, or $307,000. It is unfortunate, but unavoidable, to have such a large block item; moreover, one in which the margin of error must be particularly large, perhaps 30 per cent.

14. HOUSING

This figure is the net imputed rent, from the Income Table.

15. INCOME FROM ABROAD

This figure is the same as that in the Income Table for Remittances, together with the $90,000 estimated interest received from abroad.

VIII. GOVERNMENT ACCOUNT

Use was made, in drawing up the Expenditure Table, of two other tables which were prepared, the Government Account and the Balance of Payments.

Government Account, 1946

	$000		$000
Direct taxes, fines	637	Interest and subventions abroad	142
Indirect taxes	941	Transfer payments to the private sector of the economy	218
Income from property and profits from trading services	552	Subsidies	108
Budget deficit	298	Net current expenditure on goods and services	1415
		Capital expenditure	545
	2428		2428

The accounts of the Colony, the Belize City Council, the Town Boards and the Import Control Office were combined, excluding transfer payments between them.

Indirect taxes, taken from the Colony's accounts, are those taxes which enter into the price of an article to the consumer.

Income from property and profits from trading services include the surpluses or deficits on public utilities, etc., earnings from property and services, such as market rents, interest from investments, and earnings from the numerous services provided by Government. Some of these items might, perhaps, be more properly classed under direct taxes and fines, when the fee charged bears little relation to the cost of the service supplied. In practice all the minor services of Government were treated as earning their fees. It is very difficult to draw the line between one kind of communal service and another. Some government services seem obviously 'trading' services (and may yield profits or be subsidised), because they are services which, in some countries, are provided by private concerns. In some cases Government has a monopoly of the service and can charge more than the cost, when the excess might be considered a direct tax. In other cases less than the cost is charged, when the difference might be regarded as a subsidy. Is the registration of the birth of a child a service, and so a subsidised service? Is the fee for late registration a fine or the cost of the service? Is the fee for a copy of a birth certificate the cost of a service? Government accounts are not classified in such a way that adequate dissections can be made, even if the definitions have been agreed. It may, for example, be decided that the registration is a subsidised service, the late fee a fine and the copy of the birth certificate a service which is paid for. But these can only be disentangled by going through each entry in the accounts. In this table the definition includes all income where a service of any kind, whatever its value, has been performed apparently in direct response to, or in anticipation of, payment.

The Budget deficit bears no direct relation to the actual surplus of receipts over payments in the Colony's accounts, as grants from abroad have not been included.

Transfer payments include pensions and grants. Pensions are so treated for consistency. Pensioners, as such, have not been included in the Income and Output Tables, as they have not been classified as gainfully-occupied, unless they are so occupied under other headings. If it were desired to treat non-contributory pensions as deferred payments for services, an item would have to be added to the other two tables. This might be done by showing the pensions paid or imputing an amount to civil servants' salaries to cover a pension provision. Such treatment would hardly be sound, as pensions do not have any definite money relation to the services performed. Their money significance depends on the length of life of the pensioner. Pensions are not *earned* but *granted* in accordance with certain rules that take into account the services performed.

Capital expenditure includes all expenditure from Colonial

Development and Welfare votes. The recurrent items are small and some of them, such as training scholarships or social welfare, are really a rather intangible form of investment which is made annually.

IX. BALANCE OF PAYMENTS, 1946

	$000		$000
Value of domestic exports . . .	3513	Value of retained imports . . .	5073
Receipts from foreign missions . . .	150	Value of imported services . . .	325
Receipts from foreign property . .	40	Remittances by immigrants . . .	25
Remittances from emigrants . . .	237	Payments to foreign property-holders .	341
Net Government receipts from abroad . .	997		
Investment by foreign companies . .	827		
	5764		5764

Value of domestic exports was taken from the Customs Report.

Value of exported services, from shipping, was estimated to equal the value of imported services from the same source, and was excluded. The basis of this assumption is that, although foreign shipping services play a much larger part in the Colony's trade than domestic shipping, the receipts of foreign shipping companies operating in the Colony are largely collected elsewhere. The timber firms pay freight charges at the place where their own profits arise, and so with other concerns. The same probably applies to domestic shipping. Receipts of domestic shipping abroad were assumed to equal the payments made in the Colony to foreign shipping.

Receipts from foreign missions. This figure was arrived at by taking the net output of religion as found for the Output Table and adding the net output of education (less government grants and government education). To arrive at a figure for gross output an estimate of construction and equipment was added, by multiplying the government construction and equipment grants by four, as the missions can claim from Government 25 per cent of this expenditure. A further amount was added for hurricane reconstruction, again based on the government grant, which is roughly 58 per cent of the cost, but varies from church to church, less the actual grant itself. Ecclesiastical imports were added and the whole rounded up to include other expenses.

Output of religion			$73,427
Output of education		$140,900	
less Government grants	$98,860		
Government education	2,479		
		101,339	
			39,561
Construction and equipment		33,000	
Hurricane reconstruction		20,354	
		53,354	
less hurricane grant		11,800	
			41,554
Ecclesiastical imports			3,086
			$157,628
rounded to			175,000

on the basis of the receipts of one mission from abroad the receipts of all were calculated, proportionately, to be

$150,000

Expenditure of foreign tourists was disregarded. The Colony is fortunate in having little or no tourist trade and is spared tourists' pressure on the cost of living and the inequalities and disequilibria they produce. The expenditure of foreigners visiting the Colony was deemed equal to the expenditure of residents travelling abroad.

Income from foreign property was estimated from information supplied by the Financial Secretary.

Remittances from emigrants. This covers remittances of migrant labour and other cash gifts received. The figures were taken from the remittance accounts of the Treasury and the money and postal order accounts of the Post Office.

U.S. workers	$49,673
R.A.F.	1,675
R.A.F. tradesmen	2,878
Ex-foresters in U.K.	30,454
Imperial pensions	1,535
British postal orders and international money orders	149,263
	$235,478

Net Government receipts from abroad were taken from the Colony's accounts:

Grant-in-aid	$80,600
Interest, etc.	21,911
Other interest	2,600
Colonial development and welfare grants	350,682
	455,793
less payments abroad, public debt interest	164,558
	291,235
Armed Forces	455,900
Taxation of foreign companies (including export duties)	199,800
	$946,935

Investment by foreign companies. This covers the investment of the buying companies which finance the timber and chicle industries and the remittances of foreign shipping companies to meet local payments. It is difficult to estimate the extent of this 'investment', which to the companies is probably an expenditure item financed out of profits. The free importation of timber machinery and equipment, petrol and other supplies has been taken from the Customs Report; other information has been received of the remittances of shipping companies. The net investment by foreign companies has, from these sources, been estimated at $827,000. It is debatable whether export duties should be included under this or the previous item.

Value of retained imports has been taken from the Customs Report.

Value of imported services, excluding shipping, was taken to include air services and insurance. About 6000 passengers passed in and out of the Colony. In 1946, however, the Jamaica plane connected, by one day, with the 'Taca' services to Central America. The passenger figure was, therefore, greatly inflated.[1] The Collector of Customs estimated that 25 per cent of the outward passengers were Colony residents and paid their return fares, which would average $200. This gave a figure of $300,000 from which was deducted $75,000 to cover local expenditure by the airways companies on wages and materials. $100,000, estimated from the income tax returns, was added for the gross premiums paid to foreign insurance companies.

Remittances abroad by immigrants cover family remittances by civil servants and estimates of other remittances and leave-salaries of civil servants.

Payments to foreign property-holders were derived from the income tax returns.

[1] See Table XI.

X. EXPENDITURE, 1946

	$000	$000	$000
(1) Consumption: Food, drink and tobacco	4,522		
Clothing	1,304		
(2) Other personal and private capital expenditure	5,541		
		11,367	
(3) Less Indirect taxes		941	
		10,426	
(4) Plus Subsidies		108	
		10,534	
(5) Government expenditure on current goods and services		1,415	
(6) Government investment		545	
			12,494
(7) Remittances abroad			25
			12,519
Less Disinvestment:			
(8) Net Government receipts from abroad		947	
(9) Investment in the Colony by foreign companies		827	
(10) Income of foreign missions		150	
			1,924
			10,595
(11) Saving			212
			10,807

(1) *Consumption; and* (2) *Other personal and private capital expenditure.*

Owing to the lack of any guide to consumption habits it was not possible to estimate personal consumption in detail and independently, but only to calculate the amounts spent on food, drink and tobacco and on clothing. These figures were obtained by taking the retained imports of each. As they were net of indirect taxes and subsidies, to give the table the usual form and to indicate their effect, indirect taxes were added and subsidies deducted here, being reversed and shown separately in items 3 and 4. Similarly all other retained imports plus imported services were taken. It was not possible to separate Other Personal Expenditure from Private Capital Expenditure for lack of data. The indirect taxes were spread over the three figures in proportion, with a reduction for food, which is slightly less subject to duty. Subsidies were deducted from food. To the resultant three figures domestic output was added, less domestic exports. From the third figure (Other Expenditure) the values of the output of Commerce and of Transport and Communications were deducted and spread over all three items in order to divide the costs of distribution, with a weighting in favour of food, much of which was assumed to be taken by the producer to the consumer or eaten by the producer as consumer. In dividing the costs of distribution, however, an amount was deducted, as part of the items 'Commerce' and 'Transport and Communications' refers to the transit and export trades and does not enter into domestic expenditure. The share of distribution attributed to the transit trade was taken to bear the same proportion to the total cost of distribution as the transit trade bore to the gross trade. The share attributable to the export trade was arrived at by taking 50 per cent of all items of Transport and Communications, except Motor Transport, of which 25 per cent was taken, plus the wages paid to the local staffs of the buying firms which finance the timber and chicle industries. It seemed desirable in this table to show the full share of Government in the economy, so the expenditure of Government was deducted and shown separately in items 5 and 6.

(3) *Indirect taxes;* (4) *Subsidies;* (5) *Government expenditure on current goods and services;* (6) *Government investment.*

These figures were taken from the Government Account.

(7) *Remittances abroad* are taken from the Balance of Payments. This matches Remittances from Abroad included in the other tables. The principle used has been to include all items which increase or diminish personal incomes.

Disinvestment. (8) *Net Government receipts from abroad;* (9) *Investment by foreign companies;* (10) *Income of foreign missions.*

These three items are taken from the Balance of Payments. They represent the 'investment', government or other, capital or recurrent, in the Colony from abroad. They have not been added to the Income and Output Tables. The effect would be misleading, as they are not income due to, i.e. resulting from, resident factors of production. In any case to add them to the Income and Output Tables would involve duplication, as they would be recorded in total and again, partly, as income in the hands of individual earners.

This foreign money is partly paid out in wages, and so generates incomes, and partly buys imports directly, and so generates expenditure directly. This directly generated expenditure on imports has no connection with resident factors of production, and in the same way as the foreign money has been excluded, as separate income, from the Income and Output Tables, so the expenditure directly generated by it must be excluded from the Expenditure Table. It might be thought that by deducting the whole amount of the foreign money, not only are the imports directly generated by it being excluded, but the expenditure of the incomes generated by it as well. This is not so. The expenditure of the incomes generated by it appears twice in the total of items 1-6.

Items 1-6 consist of retained imports and retained domestic output. The latter is made up of the incomes of the persons engaged in it. We have seen from the Balance of Payments that such foreign money as comes into the Colony goes abroad again in payment of imports of goods and services and other items. The foreign money which is paid in wages, if it can be imagined as something distinct, will circulate until it finds its way back in the purchase of an import, or equivalent. It is therefore included twice, once as an import, and once as an output item which has been used to build up the expenditure items. The foreign money which directly purchases imports is only included once. Deducting the whole amount of the foreign money, or Disinvestment item, leaves only the foreign money which generates incomes, the same definition as has been used in Income and Output Tables, while the duplication and the directly generated imports have been excluded.

(11) *Saving*. This is a residual figure. There is little available information to check it. The excess of deposits over withdrawals of the Government Savings Bank was $96,000. This bank is peculiar in that it is used extensively as a current account. In view of the exchange control restrictions, which reduce the possibility of investment in the United States, the customary home of investments by the Colony's residents, permission has generally been readily given to exceed the limit of $20,000 per depositor. About half the deposits are for accounts of much over this sum.[1] It is unlikely that other savings would exceed this by much. $116,000 seems a reasonable figure for commercial bank accumulations and other savings.

If the amount of $351,000, being the income of foreign registered companies, is added to the total, the result is the net taxable income of $11,108,000. The totals of items 1-7, $12,519,000, are the nearest approach that can be got to the income of all factors of production operating in the Colony. This, however, takes no account of the profits of the 'buying' firms.

[1] See 1946 Audit Report.

XI. POPULATION AND OUTPUT

	% *Population*	% *Output*
Agriculture	29·13	14·98
Quarrying	0·04	0·02
Fishing	1·66	1·02
Forestry	13·43	21·38
	44·26	37·40
Manufacture and repair	9·37	9·20
Construction	5·35	5·45
Transport and communications	4·50	5·17
Trade and finance	8·52	15·37
Professional service (including recreation)	4·35	4·53
Public service	6·74	8·43
Personal service	9·33	2·80
Ill-defined	7·58	2·85
	100·00	91·20
Housing and income from abroad	—	8·80
	100·00	100·00

A comparison of the share in the net total output of each branch of industry with the share of the gainfully-occupied population engaged in that branch, set out in the table of Population and Output, is suggestive.

In the primary industries it shows that 29·13 per cent are engaged in agriculture and produce 14·98 per cent of the national output. Even this share is surprisingly large, in both numbers and output, in what is not thought of as an agricultural community. It is largely due to the inclusion of subsistence agriculturists and indicates a relatively untrained, potential, agricultural labour force. The immediate problem of agriculture would not seem to be shortage of labour so much as a lack of training, skill, and 'know-how' (what Prof. Pigou puts as the fourth factor of production beside Land, Labour and Capital), lack of communications and lack of capital in the form of tools. 13·43 per cent of the population is engaged in forest industries and produces 21·38 per cent of the national output. These figures are deceptive, however. 9·29 per cent of the national output is derived from the chicle industry and is income in the hands of the agricultural population. Either this amount should be added to agriculture, or the percentage of the population engaged in forest industries increased by the numbers of *chicleros* not included in the Census. Over all it can be said that in the primary industries some 44·26 per cent of the population is engaged in producing 37·40 per cent of the national output.

9·37 per cent of the population is engaged in manufacture and repair and produces 9·20 per cent of the national output. Well over half of these are small craftsmen and tradesmen working on their own account, and small employers. The high proportion engaged suggests that the pattern is a relic of more prosperous days when the community could support more of these and, in part, was a society in which the small craftsman was a more essential part of the community than he is today, when cheap articles can be imported from abroad. The man who once made shoes now only repairs shoes. The demand for shoes has been transferred not to a local factory but abroad.

This ousting of the local craftsmen is part of the pattern of industrial development everywhere. Every village in Europe that was once comparatively self-contained can tell the same tale. Whereas in an industrialised country the local craftsmen gives way to the local factory, in a dependent economy nothing replaces the handicraft worker except imports. The community becomes progressively more dependent. This, which in itself is natural and beneficial as part of the international division of labour, causes much emotional distress to social welfare enthusiasts who apply quite a lot of money to reviving or keeping alive decaying and uneconomic industries. These may retain some life when there is a tourist trade. Apart from this they can only be revived as hobbies. Otherwise the change from the local craft to the imported article is not harmful to the community, because the craftsman with his low productivity is expensive, provided that the community can increase its efficiency in the things it continues to produce and so buy a sufficient quantity of the imported articles. That is to say that in a dependent economy the craftsman is replaced not by a factory producing similar products but by an export industry producing something quite different. Other things being equal, the craftsman survives or decays according to the proportion of the export industries to all industry and to the efficiency of the export industries, to whether imports are expensive to the community in real terms or cheap.

This point illustrates very clearly the difficulties of making a national income study of a dependent economy. It is something like the study of the arm as something dependent on the body, but apart from it conceptually, having some essential core of being on its own. But the community in a dependent economy has a social essence and existence of its own. In economic terms this may be like studying the national income of Devonshire. Even Devonshire has some essential Devonshireness which is conceivable. The Hondurasness of British Honduras is, from its geographical separation and racial make-up, more real and gives some validity to treating it apart, on its own.

13·02 per cent of the population is engaged in distribution and produces 20·54 per cent of the national output. It has already been noted that transport and communications are little developed, and if their share is taken out, the share of commerce in the national income is very high. 8·52 per cent of the population is engaged in commerce and receives 15·37 per cent of the national income. It is not the proportion of the population engaged in this tertiary and unproductive industry that gives rise to comment, so much as its share in the national income. There are in retail and wholesale trade some 451 businesses which received in profits 58 per cent of the income of the trade. There were 515 salespersons employed in shops who received 23½ per cent of the income of the trade. These proportions suggest two things, when it is realised that there are 673 other persons in the trade: that the big shops have perhaps over-large staffs; and that profits are unduly high. It seems that the Colony is carrying a burden of high commercial profits which increase distribution costs and so the cost of living. These are only inferences drawn from the figures and cannot be considered as statements of fact. The high profits are partly due to shortages of supplies in the immediate post-war period, the consequent rapid turnover of stocks and the absence of competition. Partly, they are responsive to the inflationary pressures of financial help received by the Colony from abroad, and by the presence of armed forces. They do reveal the forces of inflation at work and indicate that the increase in money values resulting from inflation tends to find its way more into the hands of the commercial community than any other. That is, perhaps, why commercial communities, organisations and individuals are usually willing to support any scheme for spending public funds, as the major part will flow through their hands and the cream, as it were, can be removed.

There is, however, this to be remembered. Trade is almost the only major grouping in the Colony, organised on a capitalist basis (as opposed to a craft basis), of which the profits are included in the tables. In forestry the profits accrue abroad and are excluded, and in agriculture very little is on a capitalist basis. This accounts in part for the larger share of trade in the national income. If the profits which arise in the other industries, mainly forest, were included in the tables, the national income would be appreciably larger. This is one of the most awkward problems of a dependent economy. It depends for its livelihood on foreign capital and it must give that capital security and a good return. The more independent the area is politically the greater must be the return it gives to counter the greater risk involved. Nevertheless, the fact remains that the natural wealth of the area which is extracted by such foreign capital contributes only in part to the wealth of the community residing in the area. The part depends on how much of the local population is employed in the industry, and how much of the proceeds goes abroad, and in this way more advanced countries are able to profit from wealth which is not theirs.

Once the first benefits of investment by foreigners, in higher standards of living for the local population, have been achieved, the next stage is a demand for greater participation, and the belief that if the industry can be taken over and put into local hands, there will be a great increase in the wealth of the country. On the face of it, this is largely true, but it comes up against practical difficulties in the inexperience and lack of business connections and goodwill of the local inhabitants, and the danger of frightening away further foreign capital. It immediately raises moral and emotional problems, of to whom the benefit should go, of whether the majority of employees will be better off under a local capitalist than a foreign capitalist, of whether, if the benefit goes to the local capitalist, the country is sufficiently highly developed administratively to ensure that the benefit is spread over all and does not merely enrich the few, and round-the-corner words which cover a mass of undigested emotional attitudes like 'Socialism', 'Communism', 'Free Enterprise', are lurking, ready to bedevil any serious discussion.

It would be unprofitable to follow these arguments. One decides between them, not by tracing them through to see which accords with any first principles one may have, but according to one's own emotional make-up or nature or, perhaps more powerfully, according to what one may hope to gain out of one or the other. Many persons find no difficulty, for example, in maintaining a pro-Socialist line of argument in Britain and a pro-Capitalist line in the colonies. The wise man ceases to follow the arguments once he has recognised that they have left the rational level and are being considered at the emotional level, and simply says, 'My feelings lead me to prefer this, that or the other', if he must state a view at all. At this stage he is really an observer of the scene, and can merely assess the strength of the various emotional forces at work. All I am trying to do is to state that demands for expropriation of foreign concerns are natural, and that suspicion of foreign capital is natural. It is in the nature of things that such feelings must be aroused. The only way for the foreign capitalist to combat these emotions is by buying the emotions of a sufficient number of the influential and powerful persons in the dependent community.

Reverting to Devonshire: the problem does not arise there in the same terms. In a well-organised society the benefits of investment in Devonshire, which comes from outside Devon, will be spread over the community as a whole, including Devonshire, which will also benefit from investment in other parts of the country. In a less well-organised society the symptoms are present, and if the wealth is partly drained off with no corresponding return, local nationalism and separatism may result. The political ineffectiveness of Welsh and Scottish nationalism is due to the fact that Wales and Scotland are integral parts of a well-organised community, in which the benefits are shared by all and are attainable by all. The political effectiveness of Irish nationalism is attributable to the opposite.

It would be interesting to know how the Marxists, with their special theory of national income calculation, would deal with the trading profits of a dependent economy. They normally attribute a figure, called 'the value of the product appropriated by private trade' to the primary industry whose product is handled by trade. The basis of this principle is that the productiveness of trade, and they do consider it productive, is limited to the value of the services of the trader. In so far as his profits exceed the value of his services, that excess is the value he appropriates, and is transferred from private trade to the primary or secondary industry. If we exclude, as we have been compelled to do, the profits of foreign timber firms, part of which is 'value appropriated', the remaining traders handle, in the main, imported goods. The 'value appropriated' thus belongs only in a small part to the local primary and secondary industries, and mainly to producers abroad. In such a case it is value appropriated from consumers and not producers. Any division between consumers and producers would have to be arbitrary and would be difficult to estimate and to account for. The part attributable to consumers would presumably be deducted from national income altogether. This raises awkward problems of theory. Logically the 'transformation of the form of value', by which term the Marxist describes the change in price between the trader's buying and selling figures after deducting the costs of trade, including an imputed salary to the profit-earner, adds nothing to the national wealth, but only gives the trader a right to a greater part of that wealth. (The term 'trader' has been used throughout because I started with the trader as the only character included in this study to whom the argument applies, but elsewhere the argument applies to any other form of private enterprise.) Nevertheless, rights to wealth or, if you like, to the products of labour are important factors in an economy, admittedly more so in a capitalist than in a communist country. As long as national income calculations are designed to give an accurate picture of the whole economy and the share of the different parts in it, Marxist national income calculations, omitting, as they do, the 'non-productive' sectors, must be considered incomplete, a part only of the economy and of the national income, and less valuable, even to Marxists, than the more usual studies. It is not even that the two kinds of calculation are trying to measure two different things. Fundamentally they are measuring the same thing, but in very different terms. The normal calculation accepts the consequences of using a money notation, and makes a statement that this is the way money changes hands in a given community, and as money is the only satisfactory measure we have of the economic activities in a community, we consider this to be a fair picture of the sum of a community's economic activities. The Marxist, on the contrary, tries, while using a money notation, to make various adjustments on emotional or moral grounds. Fundamentally he says, 'I don't like this included', or 'I feel that should be shown there.' Instead of making his calculation and letting others draw the emotional and moral conclusions which suit them, he alters his figures, in effect saying, 'These are the emotional and moral conclusions which you should draw.' It is doubtful whether his national income figures are more valuable than statements of productivity and trade returns would be, using varied notations.

XII. THE FUTURE

It has been shown that the Colony has grown up by the extraction of forest produce, which was the original cause of its existence, and that immigration in the 19th century was mainly agricultural. The resources of forest and the soil are the only natural resources.

The forest resources can be extensively exploited with a comparatively small labour force and the return in relation to that labour force has been high and has enabled the Colony to maintain, by colonial standards, a fairly high standard of living. This exploitation has gone on for over 150 years without interruption, although with occasional fears that the end was in sight. The earlier period was concerned mainly with the rich returns from the extraction of logwood until that trade was finally killed by the introduction of aniline dyes. It is only for the last 150 years that the resources which are being exploited today have formed the basis of trade. The industry gradually spread until it had extracted the merchantable timber from most of the parts that were likely to be accessible even with modern transport. It spread finally over the borders of the Colony, within which it has now had to withdraw again as a result of the closing of the Guatemalan border.[1] The resources of the forest are not yet used up. The worked-out lands will regenerate themselves, but the intensity of extraction will be reduced. Attempts to market subsidiary hardwoods may mitigate the reduction slightly.[2] The complete control now

[1] 'One of the large American firms working partly in this Colony and partly in Guatemala has removed entirely to Nicaragua owing to political difficulties in Guatemala' (*Report of the Forest Department for the year ended 31st December 1948*).

[2] The extraction of other hardwoods is, however, mostly directly subsidiary to the extraction of mahogany, which alone justifies the capital expenditure involved. 'The fall in mahogany prices in the U.S.A. is attributed to an influx of mahogany at cheap prices from West Africa and renewed production in the Philippines. . . . Under these conditions there is little chance of marketing the lesser known hardwoods from the inaccessible hill areas of the Colony until an adequate road system has been built' (*ibid.*).

exercised by Government over the cutting of trees will limit the amount that can be exported in any one year. Only the natural increase will be cut. In practice, of course, other factors will enter the picture, and the amount cut in any year will depend on prices, the regions in which operations occur, and so on. Although the cutting from year to year will be variable, over a long period the average cutting should work out close to the natural increase, barring unexpected events such as a permanent fall in demand. Even the small labour force engaged in timber extraction will not, therefore, be fully required, nor can forestry be expected to absorb the natural increase in population.[1] Other employments will have to be found for persons whose only skill is in forest work.

The chicle industry is in a different position and no question of exhaustion arises. This industry has only to fear synthetic substitutes and the vagaries of a special market, which may overstock itself, as it seems to have done by the end of 1948, and is subject to all those things which affect business men in commodity dealings.[2] Output will tend to increase in times of rising prices, when speculation on a rising market will encourage buying and raise prices further. It will diminish in times of falling prices, when stocks will be held and purchases reduced, i.e. when firms are afraid to buy lest they find themselves holding large stocks on a falling market and have to take inventory losses. The more open to competition the market is the more violently will these factors affect it. The fewer the buyers and the less competitive the buying, the steadier will be the industry, but its rewards will tend to be less.

There is nearly always a small group of buyers of a primary product who are seriously interested in maintaining a steady

[1] 'In the future forestry . . . will not be able to meet the needs of all the growing population. While it should be sedulously preserved, agricultural development must . . . be regarded as essential' (*West India Commission Report*, chap. XVI, para. 66).

[2] 'There has been a fall in the exports of domestic chicle . . . due to keener competition from Far Eastern gums and synthetic gums. . . . However the prices offered to the prime chicle producers for the 1948-9 season were not far below the former season and all chicleros available have been employed' (*Report of the Forest Department for the year ended 31st December 1948*).

supply from year to year and either have forward commitments or are themselves manufacturers. In 'boom' years speculators enter the market and force prices up unnaturally, forcing the regular buyers to purchase at the high prices only to be left at the end of the season to hold their stocks in a rapidly falling market. The effective demand for the product is roughly the same, but the speculator boosts prices, which he is able to do as long as some persons *have* to buy. It was to overcome such a situation that the cocoa buyers in the Gold Coast before the war formed a buying ring, all of them offering the same price, based on cabled market prices in London and New York. As the Gold Coast supplied nearly 50 per cent of the world's cocoa, the effect was bound to be to modify the market price. The arrangement was resisted by a producers' selling strike, strongly enforced by the tribal authority of the chiefs, and for one whole season no cocoa was sold. When the producers decided to sell, Government, in order not to flood the market, limited monthly exports by a system in which quotas were granted to regular buyers. In practice, the total quotas exceeded the amount which the Colony's dock and handling facilities were physically able to export.

As, however, chicle-bleeding is not a full-time occupation, there is probably a lower limit below which it is not worth the *milpero's* while to turn *chiclero*. This will also depend on the rewards of agriculture, especially maize. There are in fact two limits, a lower limit governed by the return to be had from agriculture, which will cause a man to decide whether to plant more maize or collect chicle (this can be a conscious choice, as the price for chicle which each contractor is to pay his *chiclero* is fixed when he takes out his licence); and a lowest limit, when the *milpero* will be content with his subsistence agriculture and not be tempted into the forest even though agricultural prices are low. The factors affecting the chicle industry are many. In practice, the returns are sufficiently high to make it dominant over the agriculture which its workers also carry on. It is probably a limiting factor on agricultural production in certain areas. Unless, however, the rumours of synthetic substitutes are true, the industry does not present quite the same problems for the Colony as the timber industry, because its workers have another occupation. Indeed, in the long run, with the smallness of the population, the decay of the chicle industry might be beneficial to the Colony (thought of as the sum of its inhabitants), as agriculture would be stimulated and a larger agricultural labour force be available (not in numbers but in man-hours).

Agriculture has only come into being at all in the last hundred years,[1] and is still, to a great extent, only subsistence agriculture of a primitive kind. A banana industry rose and fell. Coconut 'production' is still responsive to high prices. Citrus is being developed on its own. Of the hindrances to agriculture the chief have been the lack of transport facilities and the vast tracts of privately owned and undeveloped land in the areas served by water transport. Very little of the agricultural population has gravitated to the Colony as a result of its natural attractions. Some have fled from danger or oppression; some have been transported; and still they are few. The Colony lacks the highly developed transport systems of modern Europe or the United States. Extending agriculture implies building roads at great cost. The Colony is suggestive of medieval Europe when it too was thinly populated and largely forest, with settlements in clearings, communication by horse and mule, wooden towns and a busy city with its small craftsmen before industrialisation had come; sailing boats moored at the riverside at Belize; rivers considered navigable if they can take boats of a draught of no more than a few feet.

Belize itself presents even more parallels, with its dependence on rain water, its open sewers, its high wooden houses and narrow streets. The internal-combustion engine is producing, slowly, a revolution in the economy. The slowness is due to the inability of the Colony to pay for road-making, which has received a fillip in the last few years from the Colonial Develop-

[1] 'At all censuses up to 1835 the population was concentrated round Belize and there is no mention of populous settlements in the northern, western or southern parts of the Colony' (*Census of British Honduras, 1946*, chap. 1, para. 7).

ment and Welfare Acts. It remains to be seen whether economic development will follow the road-building quickly enough to enable the Colony to afford to maintain the roads which are being built, or whether agricultural communities can produce enough surplus to maintain good metalled roads. We do not know whether even highly developed agricultural systems do in fact maintain their own roads, as a highly developed agriculture is usually complementary to a highly developed industrial system which probably creates and largely maintains the road system on which agriculture depends. This is natural, as the market creates the demand for the road to bring in the products which it needs. In an old economy the roads have grown and developed over hundreds of years, and current agriculture reaps the investment of centuries with only a little improvement to make. In newer industrial countries the road system tends to decline away from industry. In a purely agricultural community which aims at exporting its products, agriculture has to bear the whole cost of the system of communications and cannot pass any on to the consumer without making its prices too high. Where roads are provided as a gift, as they are made by hand and the gift takes the form of wages to labour, the effect is somewhat inflationary. Wages and prices tend to rise and export prices rise too. Anyway, means of communication are being provided to scattered settlements and new areas are being opened to settlement. Now an attack has been made on the further problem of the development of privately held land, by a graded land tax, which is designed to tax most heavily the better, undeveloped, agricultural land, and to compel its development or surrender by its present owners.[1] As these lines of action take effect it should be possible to increase the Colony's production of agricultural goods until at least the local needs in major foodstuffs are supplied, beans, rice, meat, milk, butter, lard, etc. The Colony is generally self-supporting in sugar and maize, but in years of bad harvests it has to import these too. This is because there is a negligible export of agricultural products and little inducement to increase it.

[1] See *Report of the Forest Department for the year ended 31st December 1948.*

It has already been noted that the forest industries have created a high wages-prices structure which is a sort of permanent inflation compared with the rest of the world. This is the result of the relatively high rewards of the forest industries, owing to the high prices paid for imported foodstuffs, which in turn have been due to the early lack of, and later small development of, indigenous agricultural production. It might be thought that labour was dear simply because it was scarce. This does seem to have been the case in the past and is, of course, an overriding factor in general terms today. By raising wages sufficiently high, no doubt the labour force could be increased by attracting workers from agriculture. The increase would have to be great, as agriculturists have a tradition and a vague tie with the land. The effect of lowering wages would cause labour to emigrate, as the cost of living is high. A small part might turn to agriculture, but the lack of capital would prevent most, as there is little agricultural employment. In a country dependent on expensive imported foods for feeding its working classes there are limits below which wages cannot go, provided that a labour force of a fixed size is required. Even if labour could not emigrate, there are alternative occupations, such as fishing and agriculture, on a near-subsistence basis, which would be preferable after wages had declined beyond a certain point. Government would be bound to step in and assist. In fact, from the 1931 crisis and hurricane until the outbreak of war, Government had to provide relief work for the unemployed. A large part of the Belize–Cayo road was built as relief work. During the war many found employment abroad and in the forces. Relief schemes were unnecessary. Now (1949) they have been introduced again. Relief schemes imply that labour cannot have been scarce.[1]

[1] 'The lack of sufficient industrial or agricultural development to provide employment for the growing population is the underlying cause for the unemployment which was in evidence long before the last world war began and which was temporarily solved by the full employment available during the boom years of wartime activities. Since hostilities ceased there has been the gradual return of large numbers of workers who found employment abroad, and the situation was brought to a climax during 1949 by serious recessions in the mainstay mahogany and chicle industries, coupled with a

Dear and cheap labour are relative terms. Obviously within any one economy labour may become plentiful and cheap or scarce and dear, but the levels at which dearness and cheapness are considered vary from one economy to another. African labour has been considered cheap by European standards and has enabled European-run farming to exist in East and Central Africa, where the low wage costs have made the products competitive, without great efficiency. Today, rising costs are causing even African wages to rise, and except for the growers of some products in exceptional post-war demand, European farming is subsidised. This seems partly designed to keep wages down as there is a belief that the continuance of the European position in tropical Africa depends on the lowness of wages. This is doubtful, and the reverse is more likely to be true on political grounds.

The point to be made is that British Honduras labour is dear by West Indian standards and must be dear owing to the higher cost of living. Imported food was necessary and wages had to be high to meet its cost. This discouraged any development of agriculture under the plantation, or large estate, system. The increasing supplies of tinned foods increased the dependence on imports and even affected agriculturists. The small farmer produced less variety of foods for himself, but supplemented the basic food which he grew by earnings in chicle and elsewhere. Everything, then, has combined to discourage agriculture, and it is remarkable that 29·13 per cent of the gainfully-occupied population is engaged in such agriculture as there is (see Tables of Population and Output). The methods of financing the forest industries are not inflationary in themselves, except in so far as the forest industries themselves are. The financing of government activities by grant undoubtedly does contribute to some extent to the general local inflation. Government receipts from abroad equal 9·27 per cent of the national income. Any excess of investment over saving must have an inflationary effect. In

severe drought which ruined crops and forced many small planters into wage seeking in order to earn a livelihood' (*Annual Report on the Working of the Labour Department for the year ended 31st December 1949*).

the same way the expenditure of mining companies on capital development in other colonies tends to produce pockets of inflation where wages and prices are higher than elsewhere in the same Colony. Government spending of income received from abroad must be considered as contributing to the difficulties of agriculture, but in that respect only. Clearly its other effects, such as improved communications, are directly beneficial. It is unfortunate that government capital expenditure, which is partly directed to agricultural development, is taking place in an already inflated economy instead of, as is usual, in a Colony with a low wages-prices structure where the inflation is of itself a stimulus to agriculture and a kind of pump-priming. In British Honduras the effect is stimulating up to the point where the local market is fully supplied.

Local inflation. It is too often generally believed that inflation in the colonies is a product of something that happens in the outside world and that local policies or actions have no bearing on it. On a large view this is, of course, true. All colonies depend to a large extent on imports of a wide range of consumer and capital goods. When there is inflation elsewhere prices are higher in the Colony. This creates many problems for a colony, but they are not, strictly, problems of inflation for that colony. It is an aspect of dependence. The high proportion of the national expenditure in a dependent economy which goes on imports gives an air of unreality to treating it as a separate economy at all. As far as capital goods are concerned, in the private sector of the economy they are not even problems for the Colony, as the proportion of local capital available for investment is usually negligible and private investment depends on outside finance. This is to a less, but still predominant, extent true of government investment, which depends on loans raised or grants received, and may contribute to inflation elsewhere, but, in so far as it is spent on capital goods, not locally.

In the post-war world there have been exceptional factors, arising from the fact that it is a post-war world, which have accentuated local inflationary problems. Owing to the direct link with sterling of nearly all colonial currencies through their currency boards, the colonies have access to a supply of foreign capital or money, which is limited only by the availability of objects of profitable investment and the willingness of persons to invest in a colony. There is a further limitation on the exceptionally large investment owing to the control of capital issues in London, but this has a relatively small effect in the present context,

It will be convenient to assume for the moment that there is no inflation or deflation going on in the outside world. The war has just ended and the moral purpose behind price controls is weakening; merchants are chafing at controls and the public is thinking again in terms of a pre-war world. In this situation governments are encouraged to promote development schemes, and money is made available for them. This was the main factor in British Honduras. In other colonies private investment together with immigration were large additional factors. Wartime reserves were released and the raising of public loans permitted. There was thus a great deal of money, in local terms, available for spending. It is doubtful if, in all, it would have any marked effect on world prices. It is not necessary for inflation that money should be actually in circulation, but merely that it should be available and that there should be an eager desire to spend it. This situation existed in nearly all colonies, and produced a pressure on goods and prices.

Some of the pressure thus created was for imported goods, actual capital equipment, or, at one remove, on consumer goods, through the employment of local labour on projects and their wish to buy imported goods. In a situation where the imported goods were in plentiful supply and only required a local demand to be forthcoming, this pressure would not be inflationary. For example, the large investment of American firms in capital goods purchased in the U.S. was not inflationary at all. This argument applies to all the money which was spent directly in other countries. In the case of goods purchased through merchants in the colony, however, there were inflationary effects. These were not great, but were real. In the post-war situation goods never became readily available. The producing countries had not fully recovered from the dislocation caused by the war to their industries and the supplies only began to become readily available in 1949, with a resultant fall in prices in goods from the U.S., where the economy made a more rapid and fuller recovery. This temporary American 'recession' caused a lowering of the cost of living index in Belize up to the time when the British Honduras dollar was devalued. It is interesting to note that a situation which ceased to be inflationary was termed a 'recession' and it suggests a peculiar and rather sectional approach to economics. It is perhaps natural that, in a world where the merchant and industrialist make the economic wheels go round, any reduction in their returns should be a 'recession', while it is a boon to the man who buys their products and for whom, in theory, the economic system works. On the whole, however, pressure was exerted on local merchants, owing to their inability to provide the goods demanded in the quantity demanded. They were themselves used to a period when goods were in short supply during the war, and to a time when their profit margins were protected by price control and the saleability of everything they stocked ensured that they bore no losses, and they had not recaptured the habits of competition. In general, then, one might say that the availability of money in so far as it presses on imported goods is not normally inflationary, but was so in the exceptional post-war world, when imported goods were not themselves available in sufficient quantities.

The main effect of ready money takes place in the local economy. Most colonial economies are mainly agricultural. Certainly the local supply of consumer goods consists of agricultural products. Agriculture is much slower to respond to economic changes than most sectors. It is not easy for agricultural production to be stepped up rapidly to meet a greatly increased demand. This is particularly so when the agriculture is relatively primitive and the capitalisation of the country in communications is under-developed. Instead of a gradually increasing demand met by a gradually increasing production, and equilibrium maintained, there is a greatly increased demand and a very slowly responding production. When the money available for investment goes chiefly in wages, as it tends to do the more backward the country is, and money is spent on basic things like roads and not on imported capital goods, the pressure is all the greater. It is still greater in a primitive and poor society because an inadequately nourished population will tend to increase its purchases of food. To a lesser degree the same forces affect the usual small colonial secondary industries, the ubiquitous cigarette and soap factories, etc. In this way there is a local inflation entirely separate from any world inflation and additional to it. In a large colony, with considerable areas given over to subsistence agriculture and concentrations of development in certain areas, this local inflation may occur in localities only and not over the colony as a whole.

On the assumption that supply would catch up with demand at some point, inflation would cease and a new equilibrium be attained; an equilibrium in which social relations would be different and the economic relations of classes changed, but nevertheless an equilibrium. In such a context the political problems of inflation are short-term, designed to alleviate distress and smooth the transition to the new order. In a society where the inflation affected all simultaneously and equally there would be no problems of adjustment. In fact, inflation is marked by the increase in wealth of one class, e.g. the merchants, and, in colonies which are receiving exceptionally high prices for some primary commodities, certain farming groups, and the impoverishment of the rest. If this were the only problem that had to be guarded against it could be done, with difficulty no doubt, but with a measure of success. Unfortunately it does not seem to be recognised as a problem in those terms, and its solution awaits discontent, strikes, and action by the sufferers. When that happens there has been a failure of policy. Many governments conduct their economic and political policies in watertight compartments.[1] When trade is booming and many

[1] This is perhaps a product of the indeterminate specialisation which is common today. The emphasis is on analysis and more analysis, experts in smaller and smaller subdivisions and yet more experts; but no synthesis. Synthesis is left to the Marxists and the Roman Catholics, who have a logical

people are getting richer, it is apt to be forgotten that even more are getting poorer, and a sharp reminder is needed from the impoverished that policy has been neglected. Although inflation may be a short-term problem, economically it may have very long-term political effects unless there is a positive short-term policy for dealing with it (either by restraining it or by mitigating promptly its effects). In the disequilibrium produced by inflation new political aspirations take shape, new political leaders arise who have a mass of discontented and dissatisfied people to work on. If the leaders are resolute and intelligent, far-reaching and permanent political concessions may be wrung from a government that had no intention, or thought, of conceding anything two years earlier. I am not suggesting that the new political leaders are not sincere. Some may join a movement who have no more interest than to further their own advancement. Such do not achieve great political changes. The trouble is that they arise from specific situations and the political changes they advocate are not necessarily, and indeed seldom, those which are required for dealing with the specific situation that created them. In any event, even if what they advocate is correct for the situation, a permanent political change results from what is a short-term problem. Instead of political changes taking place for sound reasons of policy, designed to maintain the equilibrium and happiness of the society, they take place in an atmosphere of emotion and are based on shibboleths and slogans. No one stops to consider what, if any, benefits may be expected to accrue from them.

As far as exports are concerned in such an inflationary situation, a colony which is already at a disadvantage is rendered still more so. Without considering, for a moment, the report of

framework on which to base their specialisations. But there is no 'democratic' synthesis. In the liberal world each specialist judges things outside his specialisation by it. The result is confusion. This is particularly true of policy where the essential wholeness of, and mutual interdependence within, a society is overlooked. It is true in another sense in an under-developed society, which needs less of the experts who have been trained in a rather special environment, and who are exported with their inculcated ideas to the very different environment of the colonies in increasing numbers, and more of the synthesists, the jacks-of-all-trades, the adaptors.

the Evans Commission it would seem that government policy must in the first place be directed towards the development of agriculture, in view of the likely diminution of production in the forest industries, and that it should be aimed, apart from development of communications and the encouragement of agriculture on private land, which are already in hand, at improving methods of agriculture and seed strains, at introducing better implements, and at fostering production for the local market by the existing population. A country in which 29·13 per cent of the population is engaged in agriculture should not be so dependent on outside food supplies. Admittedly the population is scattered, but the main internal markets are fairly concentrated. This will imply some diversification of agriculture, the encouragement of one crop at the expense of another, the introduction of new crops. It can partly be effected by the judicious fixing of prices by the Marketing Board, but that cannot cover the whole field, as the Board does not purchase more than a fraction of the different kinds of agricultural produce. It does not deal in meat products at all. In any event the Colony, which is really a very small market, cannot afford the overheads of such an organisation to deal with even as much as is being dealt with now. It interposes a new and expensive middleman into the costs of distribution, which, as has been seen, are already high. The main hope would seem to lie in the organisation of farmer's co-operatives. On these Government might bring persuasion to bear to have its policy carried out and any attempt at executing policy through prices could be carried out more effectively and cheaply.[1] Direct interference would be too expensive and would probably contribute to the inflationary effect. In parenthesis it may be regretted that the new Marketing Board, which is a separate organisation on its own with all the extra expense that that implies, has replaced the old Board of Agriculture, which was really the Agricultural Department under another name, and

[1] In Kenya, the Kenya Farmers' Association is a major instrument by which Government carries out its policy. There is, of course, interaction, and it might be said that the Association both affects and effects Government policy.

carried out a policy of price-supporting some half-dozen commodities through the 'machinery' of the Department, which exists throughout the Colony and was supplied free, spare-time.

Side by side with this purely agricultural policy, a policy aiming at lowering the wages-prices structure would be necessary, with the more distant aim in view of agricultural production for export. In the short term self-sufficiency, or something approaching it, would be aimed at. In the long term, when a stable and varied agriculture had been built up, based on the local market, then production for export would be needed. The local market is really extremely small. This is a point that is often overlooked by local planners or would-be planners, who, on the principle that 'the Smiths have it, so why can't we', and 'you must keep up with the Browns', want to introduce all kinds of wonderful schemes into a situation in which they would have very little function. (In a country where the magazine *Time* is widely read, the Smiths and the Browns tend to be the United States.) The agricultural potential of the country, even with its present population, if fully extended with only moderate improvements in methods, would soon outstrip the local market. Any policy aiming at supplying the local market would, then, be a very short-term policy indeed. Even without settlers from outside the matter of production for export would soon arise, if only as a question of disposing of surpluses. It is assumed that the forest industries will continue to bring in appreciable returns during the period necessary to establish agricultural self-sufficiency. Eventually agricultural exports will have to replace forest exports, or partly so, if the timber industry is to be reduced to the cutting of only the natural increase each year and the chicle industry to disappear before the competition of synthetic substitutes as the logwood industry did. Otherwise only subsistence agriculture can survive. On all these assumptions some lowering of prices and wages is necessary. Wages may be lowered 'naturally', i.e. with great hardship, distress and unemployment, by the decline of the forest industries.[1]

[1] They can be lowered by opening the Colony freely to immigration; i.e. by increasing the pressure of labour on wages and so reducing them. This would result in a great decrease in the standard of living, as there is not the

It is, no doubt, a counsel of perfection to say that this should be foreseen and guarded against or prevented. Fortunately the development of agriculture for the local market will in itself have a disinflationary effect. As the market gets saturated with successive products, prices, although still fluctuating according to harvests, should over the years tend to get lower. It will be a stiffer battle to overcome local preferences for imported foods, tinned milk, tinned butter, etc., as against the equivalent local product. It is here that a bargain might be struck with producers whereby strong protection was given to local produce in return for control of the prices of the protected products. The aim of this form of protection would be not to look after high cost industries but to discourage consumer taste. It should not, therefore, be difficult to devise a formula which would equate internal prices with world prices. Protection by itself would only increase the inflation by increasing costs and causing wages to rise. It would be necessary, therefore, until local production of any commodity had caught up with local demand, to apply a gradually increasing tariff to the protected commodity, related to the share of the locally produced commodity in the total local consumption of that commodity. Tariffs on imported foodstuffs, which enter into working-class diets and which do not compete with local produce, might be removed entirely with the aim of lowering the cost of living and reducing money wages without reducing real wages. The more important of the recently negotiated wage agreements provide for alterations corresponding to variations in the cost of living index.

This discussion of these points has been confined to the Colony as it is and on the assumption that it gets the same kind of help as it does now. It has been concerned with development from a certain point in a certain community. It is interesting to consider the *Evans Commission Report* in this con-

employment available, and a general emigration would probably ensue. The Colony can freely admit peasant farmers who would increase production, but the admission of labourers would increase unemployment. The aim is to lower wages and prices together, without affecting the standard of living, which is none too high.

text, that is, from the point of view of the Colony's present inhabitants and prospects.

The Evans Commission, specifically enquiring into the possibility of settling persons from the West Indies and elsewhere in British Honduras, looked primarily at the untapped or underdeveloped resources of the country with a view to seeing how many could be successfully settled. They were not considering settlement in subsistence agriculture or even agriculture for the local markets, but they looked for specific agricultural exports. They then considered how these items could best be developed so as to absorb as many immigrants as possible. Even if their proposals do not contribute much to the solution of the problem of West Indian overpopulation, they are revolutionary in British Honduras.[1] In the first place they considered it essential that immigration should take place under very favourable conditions, with good housing and community services provided. This entails considerable capital expenditure in any settlement scheme. They recognised the problem of high labour costs, which would continue if their proposals were carried out, as they would contribute little to the question of the Colony's self-sufficiency in agriculture. They therefore turned from the policy of the pre-war West India Commission, which had recommended the encouragement of mixed peasant farming, to what was both an older and a newer structure, the large-scale plantation using indentured labour but based on modern mechanised agriculture.

There is not necessarily a conflict in the attitudes of the two

[1] It is, however, interesting that they came to quite different and conflicting conclusions on a matter of, presumably, ascertainable fact. The *West India Commission* (chap. IV, para. 1) states: 'Considerably more than one-half of the total area of all these Colonies is forest and the use of much of the remainder for agricultural purposes is made impossible by the nature of the soil. Nowhere can there be found any substantial area of agriculturally useful land which is not already in cultivation, and in all the Colonies the density of population in relation to cultivable land is high.' The only conclusion one can draw from this statement, which is simply not true of British Honduras, where the ancient Mayans appear to have cultivated the greater part and which, it has been estimated (on how good grounds I do not know), in those days carried a population of over a million, is that the West India Commission was not very interested in the problems of British Honduras.

commissions; they are answers to quite different problems.[1] In the terms in which the problem was conceived the Evans Commission's proposals are the obvious answer. They are modern in the sense of according with the mood and fashion of the moment. They recognised, too, that one of the problems which had been overlooked in the previous highly capitalised schemes in the Colony, the cohune industry, the starch factory, the lobster-canning industry, was the maintenance of a steady and plentiful flow of raw materials. When proposing a sugar factory with ten times the output of the present one they therefore provided for a sufficient plantation system to supply it.

[1] 'Another point at which general policy should aim is the increase of the best types of existing holding in preference to the development on a large scale of any form of holding hitherto unknown in the territory' (*West India Commission*, chap. XVI, para. 15). One is tempted to heartily endorse this on social rather than economic grounds. To propose a violent change in the social structure of a society, and a structure which has attractions and develops a healthy spirit of self-reliance, would seem to be inviting a host of social and semi-political troubles. One of the biggest problems in Africa, and which has hardly been tackled, is that social institutions and ways of living adapt themselves to a changed economic environment slowly. In the process a social 'gap' occurs, when the old ways have become obsolete and new ways have not matured, in which revolutionary politics tend to enter. The social strivings of the individual find no outlet and their place is taken by emotional yearnings of any kind, which, in the hands of a few forceful 'leaders', take the common forms of class and race and colour hatred. It is not so much social welfare as social institutions that are needed to fill the gap. These are not easily constructed. To create a stable, contented society, economic and social development must go hand in hand. Over-rapid economic development (i.e. more rapid than the social adjustment) produces as many and as great strains as too slow development. What one fears for British Honduras, where many races rub shoulders fairly easily, is what one sees in Africa, where little practical sociology, the adaptation of existing institutions, the grafting on of new ones and the pruning of old ones, is attempted outside tribal areas, and where, even there, only rarely is the need for such adaptations seen. Even in West Africa, where the tribal system had to some extent been adapted to town life, the need for further adaptation to meet and absorb the new African appears to have been ignored. With the outstanding exception of the late Godfrey Wilson's studies of the urban African in Northern Rhodesia, modern sociology or anthropology, whichever it chooses to call itself, seems to confine itself either to rural studies of disappearing societies, as with the number of recent studies financed by Colonial Development and Welfare funds in East Africa, or to studies in the United Kingdom, where the practical application is likely to be nil. (Certainly this will be true if, as I have heard, a recent study of absenteeism amongst miners attributed it to the fact that they work stooping, and so in a 'foetal position'.)

Their main proposals were concerned with development of the sugar industry, of a dairying industry, revival of the cocoa industry, which had existed at the beginning of the present century until defeated by West African competition, and other lesser projects. As far as the local population was concerned it was regarded only as increasing, in so far as it could and would, the contribution of raw materials to factory or dairy. The whole of the proposals were to be carried out by the Colonial Development Corporation, with the participation of local capital, which provision seems to have been designed as a sop to local feeling, as the participation of local capital in enterprises of this size must be negligible. This was, perhaps, an attempt to compromise with the local fear of exploitation of a country's resources by others, noted earlier. The agricultural soundness of the Commission's proposals can only be judged by agriculturists; they need and are receiving considerable experimental work before being put in hand. Several purely agricultural experiments are being conducted by Government now on behalf of the Colonial Development Corporation. Economically the proposals can only be judged by experiment, too, and will no doubt need plenty of adaptation and revision to meet the actual circumstances which arise. On the face of them they are sound and on the lines of agricultural development elsewhere. It is possible to suggest some rather tentative criticisms. Costs have probably been underestimated. They usually are. Even if they are not when a plan is conceived, they often are by the time it is put into action.

The Commission has perhaps also been affected by the rather rosy appearance of post-war commodity markets and may not have given sufficient regard to their possibly being far less rosy in the future. The larger the scale of the plan, the more, in an export industry, the scheme is affected by variations in world trade. It is possible that too little attention has been paid to the lack of elementary capital development, in roads, etc., which afflicts all under-developed economies, which is different in those countries where large-scale, mechanised agriculture has been introduced, and which have not been provided out of the resources of agriculture in those countries. It usually needs a very rich return, such as mines provide, for this sort of investment to be worth while. Such criticisms as these are very tentative, because the proof of the pudding must be in the eating, and no one can say with certainty what the outcome will be. The best advice has been taken; outline plans have been carefully drawn up; careful experimentation is being carried out.

In theory the proposals of the Evans Commission are not inimical to the present population and could be considered as complementary to the outlines of agricultural development suggested earlier. The local agricultural population should benefit from the increased markets provided, both for products for the factory (and, at a stage removed, export) and for an increased demand for foodstuffs for consumption. The population would be expected to increase by 100,000. The danger is that local agriculture will not advance rapidly enough to keep pace with the new plantations. The local people will become, as it were, poor relations of the immigrants in their model houses, with their model village services and paid a daily wage. These high costs of the plantation system are intended to be offset by the high returns of organised and mechanised agriculture. Can the indigenous agriculturists, as such, survive in these conditions? or will they drift into paid agricultural employment? The new immigrants in their turn will be very tied to the plantations and, even when their indentures had expired, would have nothing else to turn to if they wished. It would be unfair to suggest that this smacks of a new slavery, and the introduction into British Honduras, which is largely a country of independent workers who can turn their hands to many things, of the conditions which have been the curse of the West Indies, a labouring agricultural population closely tied to world trade. After all, the greater control exercised over economic life in these days may be successful in ensuring some stability in world trade, especially the vulnerable agricultural commodity markets. But, on a less harsh plane than that, the 'industrialisation' of agriculture must always bring with it new, or different, social relationships, new tensions and new political strife. Change and adaptation are necessary for survival, but the aim should be to bring them about while maintaining equilibrium.

To be pessimistic for a moment, let us suppose that world agricultural markets shrank. What would happen to the labourers that produced the unwanted commodities? They would be unable and unlikely to revert to near-subsistence farming, but would look for support from the rest of the community. The rest of the community would be a handful of peasant farmers, fishermen and small craftsmen. This is the weakness of a purely agricultural community. It has nothing to fall back on, if it depends on exports and they fail. It is not the danger of a fall in prices, as long as there is some demand, but of a failure in demand. Unless it is simply exporting its own surplus or produces a sufficiently wide variety of agricultural products (other than basic foods) so that there is always some demand, it will suffer acutely, no matter how efficiently it is organised.[1] To create the conditions in which such a misfortune would have its maximum effect seems dangerous, to say the least, unless there is no alternative. The alternative would be to provide for assisted settlement within the present pattern.

It is, however, easy to ask any number of doubting questions and, as (I believe it was) Lenin said, 'A fool can ask more questions in five minutes than a wise man can answer in five days.' It can at least be safely said that the proposals contained in the Report of the Evans Commission, if carried out, will effect a social and economic revolution in the Colony. Instead of a population in which nearly half of the gainfully-occupied are

[1] It is as well, in these days of large-scale ideas, to bear in mind the remarks of the *West India Commission* (chap. XVI, para. 3): 'Crops produced for export are in jeopardy from many causes, including climatic fluctuations, such as drought [e.g. 1949—the sugar export of that year came from the pre-drought crop] and hurricanes, and loss of those crops when, as is often now the case, they are intended to pay for essential food imports, may clearly be disastrous. . . . In time of war or other major disturbance their lines of communication would be liable to attack; [cf. the extinction of citrus exports in the last war] experience has shown that a general economic crisis, or even a great decline in the world price of their exports, adversely affects the interests of communities which are too small to exercise much influence on world trade.'

independent farmers, tradesmen, etc., working on their own account, the overwhelming majority will be wage-earners. Some of the likely effects of this can be known from the study of other communities.[1] It raises the question, which most fiercely divides peoples today and which is far outside my province, of whether a community must organise itself in this highly integrated, but dangerous, way in order to survive (dangerous because the higher the degree of integration the more the whole depends on the well-being of the parts, and because the organism contains the seeds of its own decay in over-organisation, atrophy and a too rigid structure to be adaptable); or whether it can survive in the more loose and haphazard structure of *laissez-faire* capitalism, which implies less efficiency from duplication of services and wastage of the capital of failures, and has a rather immoral basis, being founded on the vice of avarice. Are we to see in the future not an industry or a trade outmoded and shed, as a dead branch may be shed by a tree, but a community outmoded because its structure is unable to adapt itself to new conditions, as certain kinds of animals have disappeared altogether?

[1] If the immigrants do no more than, or fail to, maintain themselves by their work, i.e. if the schemes are run at a loss or no profit, then the Colony gains nothing, because the exports go only to maintain the additional population. Any loss, which would presumably have to be borne by the United Kingdom, would be so much added to the price which the United Kingdom would pay for the produce or a subsidy by the United Kingdom to whoever bought the produce. Unless the schemes are profitable, there is no gain to the community, and then only to the extent to which the profits are retained or ploughed back.

XIII. THE ROLE OF GOVERNMENT

The Government is responsible for 18·22 per cent of the national expenditure: 5·07 per cent capital; 13·15 per cent recurrent. This excludes expenditure on the armed forces. The inclusion of this item would increase the Budget deficit by $456,000 and increase the government's participation in the economy to nearly 23 per cent, nearly a third of which is met by grants from abroad in one form or another. The Government Account is drawn up on somewhat different principles from the figures in the National Income Tables and the Balance of Payments and the figures do not tally always. It has been used to arrive at the share of Government in the national expenditure only. For example, taxation of foreign companies is not specifically included in the Government Account, but as part of Direct Taxation.

It is not proposed to analyse government revenue and expenditure. That would be beyond the scope of this study. It may, however, be pointed out that government revenue increased from $1,246,000 in 1939 to $2,206,000 in 1946, or by 77 per cent, and in the same period government expenditure increased from $1,539,000 to $2,552,000, or by 66 per cent.[1] This resulted in the continuance of the deficit at about the same magnitude. The actual figures are more significant than the percentages. One would expect expenditure on goods in wartime to increase more rapidly than revenue, and expenditure on services to increase less rapidly. Revenue increases as a result of increased Customs collections from higher-priced wartime goods and the taxation of increased wartime profits. (Even the same percentage profit on an article produces higher profits as the value of the article is higher and scarcity produces a more rapid turnover of available goods. The return on the same capital outlay—fewer goods but more expensive ones—comes in

[1] See Table XIII.

more frequently.) Taxation lags behind expenditure on goods, but shortages reduce the actual quantities imported by Government. There is a further time lag before wages in business proceed on their way to try to catch up with increased prices. This time lag further increases profits. The delay of earnings in following prices is especially marked with civil servants' salaries, which, in fact, never seem able even to keep prices in sight.

During the war government expenditure on goods would be less, owing to shortages (in fact, Colonial Development and Welfare expenditure fell in the war years, in 1942 to $11,000); one would expect a reduction in a colonial government's total expenditure and the building up of revenue reserves. By 1946, salaries, which accounted for 37 per cent of expenditure (and which do not include wages), had received increases of around 40 per cent. Instead, however, of government expenditure being reduced, it was increased. This is due to the fact that colonial revenue collection tends to be rather rigid. Budgeting consists in seeing how many (very much needed) services there is money available for. Revenue is collected on traditional patterns, with a general tendency over the years to increase sources and rates of taxation. This tendency has been greatly increased in recent years under pressure from the Colonial Office. Colonies are now accustomed to much higher taxation than was usual before the war. Apart from this, special war-time taxes were imposed on various self-denying, emotional grounds. In any colony there are always innumerable services lacking which jostle each other in the queue at Budget time for anything left over from the revenue.[1] As well as this, under-manned departments are always trying to expand to provide better services. (There is also a psychological tendency of heads of departments to increase their departments.) The depriva-

[1] This is not true of all colonies, even those that do not provide many services, as expenditure is often largely traditional too. New services are only introduced under pressure, or to be fashionable and give the Colony an appearance of *chic*. In Northern Rhodesia and Kenya, for example, reserves were built up during the war, although the territories do not supply even the services with which British Honduras supplies its people, as a large part of the population is not vocal.

tions of wartime induce a kind of dreamland counterweight, in which the post-war world is looked forward to as a time when cherished plans and ideas will be fulfilled. Not all colonies endured great deprivations, but any lack on that score was made good by positive inducements from the Colonial Office to plan for the post-war world, to prepare for demobilisation, and so on. In this atmosphere budgeting took place in the traditional way. Revenue was coming in better than before and there was more money to spend. The extra money was spent.

It is curious that a grant-in-aid was always needed, though never a large one. It would seem that the persistence of the grant-in-aid is partly due to a mental acceptance of the idea of a permanent grant. Budgeting takes place in an atmosphere of so much revenue available—*plus* so much grant. Efforts are made from time to time to eliminate it, but the budgeting is so narrow that there is always expenditure hanging over from the previous year and not provided for in the current year, which is sufficient to unbalance the account. In any case, in times of rising prices, estimates made in one year are almost bound to be underestimates when the expenditure is incurred in the following year and supplementary votes will be needed.

The effect of all this has been to create a structure of government which is too large for such a small population to carry (not too large for the work it is expected to do). The revenue in 1946 was one-fifth of the national income and was about $37 per head of the population.[1] This was a higher average than in the majority of West Indian colonies, except ones like Trinidad, which have mineral production to tax. It is hardly politically possible to reduce government expenditure. The main services, besides Public Works Construction, chiefly road works financed by Colonial Development and Welfare grants, were Public Works maintenance and medical, educational and police services. It has already been noted how necessary roads are to the Colony's agricultural development (and how little necessary they were

[1] Kenya, with an estimated population of 5 million, has a budget of £12 million, excluding the E.A. High Commission services; at the same rate per head as British Honduras it would have a £46 million budget.

for forest development). The roads now being built with Colonial Development and Welfare funds are laying up a future maintenance bill beyond the Colony's means. It should, within a few years, be well equipped with roads. For that reason a large increase in the population (assuming it to be productive) is necessary to enable an agricultural community to maintain them.

The Colony is already very well supplied, by colonial standards, with medical and educational services. Compulsory education is not only on the statute-book, it is largely effective. Nearly all the population is within reach of a doctor. The services are widely spread, even though there are no model hospitals or schools. There are no 'show places'. On the other hand the services are not complete. Certain kinds of specialist medical attention have to be obtained abroad, and so do certain kinds of education. This is reasonable. One does not separate Puddlecombe-in-the-Mud from the rest of the British economy and insist that it has its own university and a complete medical specialist service.

This is again the problem of the small, dependent economy,[1] and of whether limited services should be provided for all or more complete services for a few. In any event it is not politically practicable to reduce these services. The purely administrative services are always proportionately much larger in a small place than in a large one. They are the 'overheads'; the smaller the country the less it can provide out of taxation over and above its overheads.[2] This again suggests the need for productive immigrants to spread the overheads. It also suggests joining up with other larger territories with more resources.

[1] One may wonder whether, if the whole of Central America were a British possession, any Colonial Development and Welfare funds would be devoted to that part which is now British Honduras. The fragmentary nature of the British Empire often causes the spending of inadequate funds in trying to stimulate activity in an area which might be better abandoned. The administration of the Colonial Development and Welfare funds suffers from the compartmentalised nature of the Colonial Empire which has resulted from *the haphazard way in which it has been acquired*.

[2] This was brought out very clearly in my study of the accounts of Native Treasuries in Northern Rhodesia. See 'Native Treasuries in Northern Rhodesia' in the *Journal of the Rhodes-Livingstone Institute*, no. 2.

This may give greater strength in international trade bargaining, but would be offset by the larger unit tending to ignore the special needs of its smaller parts. Would British Honduras have a bigger voice in international trade negotiations if represented only as part of, say, a greater West Indies, than if represented directly or, as a unit, by the Colonial Office? Otherwise unification must depend on the larger partner having a surplus to share and so bearing part of the expenses of the smaller. If it has no surplus and poorer services than the smaller, then there seem to be no advantages. The only hope, then, of balancing the Budget is by the strictest economy, the pruning of existing services where possible and the elimination of new services. The last may seem very unfashionable, and, apart from lessening the inflationary effect of receipts from abroad in a Colony needing disinflation, raises the point of when government development expenditure should take place.

It is usual in the colonies today to think in terms of development and spending. (Sometimes it seems like spending for spending's sake.) The prospects of a slump, and the possible abandonment of all these fine schemes, is in the back of most men's minds, but it is kept firmly there and never allowed to the front. Since the 1931 crisis a lot has been written about government policy in correcting slumps (and booms). It has been said that the business man's pessimistic outlook in a downward movement of trade, when he stops investing in machinery, or inventories in anticipation of a fall in prices, which he helps to create by his action, can to some extent be corrected by government action in undertaking development and public works schemes. The effect would be to create a demand for goods and services and to replace, temporarily, private investment by government investment, relieve unemployment and create new personal incomes. The corollary of this is that a boom tendency should also be corrected by the withdrawal of government expenditure in those times. This would reduce inflationary pressures, on both goods and wages, and restrain the excesses of the boom. Thus the variations would be evened out and some stability achieved in the economy.

The practice seems rather different from the theory as far as the colonies are concerned. At a time when businesses are being re-equipped after a long and destructive war, when there are arrears of consumers' durable goods to be made up, when there are war debts to be paid out of the products of industry; at a time when there is an enormous unsatisfied demand which must produce boom and inflationary effects, one finds colonial governments not building up reserves nor trying to steady inflationary pressures, but encouraged with grants and subsidies to add to them, to join in the demand for goods and services, for commodities and labour, to undertake construction at the most difficult and expensive time and to make it more expensive by so doing. It would seem that governments are subject to that optimism which infects business men in booms, and that a public works policy properly carried out and aimed at attaining some economic stability is simply not practical politics. Assuming that no other major mishaps occur, that the dislocations of world trade are set right, and so on, then a time must come when *urgent* demand is sated and business prices and wages will have to readjust themselves to 'normal' conditions, if 'normality' will ever recur. That will show itself in a slump or 'recession' to a greater or lesser degree. It will affect colonies all the more violently because governments have contributed to the height of the boom and have no reserves to meet the recession of activity and with which to check it. This is quite apart from the fact that many colonial development schemes are being set in motion at a time of high prices and will be saddled with high capital costs which may cause them, to say the least, to make heavy weather in different times.

Many have already drawn attention to the high share which welfare takes in expenditure under the Colonial Development and Welfare Acts. It is possible to argue that welfare expenditure by grant is wholly bad, as a kind of 'bread and circuses' which will sap the morale of colonial peoples. Really it depends on the attitude of the British taxpayer as expressed by his representative. Welfare expenditure by itself will be recurrent for ever, unless sufficient development takes place for the Colony to take over the expenditure. If the United Kingdom is prepared to subsidise these welfare services indefinitely, well and good. Most welfare expenditure is, admittedly, expected to make some rather intangible contribution to development. The large share of welfare is, no doubt, partly due to the fact that welfare schemes are easier to think of than productive enterprises. But an ounce of development is worth a pound of welfare. An industry successfully established contributes more to the health and well-being of a people than any welfare directly applied. If development is looked after, welfare will look after itself. If the productivity of a colony is increased, it can provide for its own welfare which will, anyway, be thereby increased.

In British Honduras this places one in a dilemma. On the one hand the Colony urgently needs capital development to offset a declining, or at least stagnant, forest industry. On the other hand it wants a deflation to enable it to export its goods competitively. Any way out of the dilemma must be a compromise. The answer is probably that the money available should be spent on research in the first place, and secondly on pilot settlements within the present agricultural pattern, coupled with road development. A primitive agriculture and forest exploitation have revealed little of the potentialities of the country. They may be none other than are at present being used. This is very unlikely, but even this would be worth knowing. A large part of the Colony is virtually unexplored. Such exploration as has taken place has been in mahogany hunting and has revealed that at one time the Colony carried a much greater agricultural population than today. The kind of agriculture practised reveals little of the possibilities of the soil. This is one of the dangers of any large-scale investment programme in agriculture. It would be a speculation made almost wholly in the dark. There are plenty of pointers to the direction which investigation and research should take, such as the indigenous cocoa trees, which have attracted attention again lately. Mineral potentialities are completely unknown. This is again the problem of the under-developed territory with no capital to undertake research. The politically independent territory has to rely on commercial research, which is usually confined to a search for mineral wealth, which alone is considered as giving an adequate return. If it is successful it can result in either the provision, by the increase in wealth, of further local research into other possibilities; this depending on the territory being able to extract from the foreign capitalist's income from his investment a reasonable share, otherwise he produces only wage income in the hands of his workers, which will not provide a margin for saving; or it can result in the increased wealth of a few locally, owners of property, traders, etc., a certain amount of local inflation and eventually the relative depression of the workers' standards. Capital investment in British Honduras was productive of wage income, but nothing else. The income from the investment left the country either directly, or later when the capitalist removed himself to more congenial surroundings.[1] His intention to do so, if he could, would preclude his making any other investment, either social, scientific, or even for his personal comfort, in the Colony.

The politically dependent territory is fortunate, at least in these days, in having the resources of a larger economy to lean on, both in technical knowledge and skill and in capital. The quickest way to relieve any burden in dependence is by research which will reveal the full potentialities of the dependent territory. This will often be no more than repaying a debt to the descendants of the workers who produced an earlier contribution to the wealth of the mother country and whose creation they are as a result of that early exploitation.

There are two ways in which research can be undertaken; one relatively fast and painless, 'soft' research, by the lending or giving of money for specific research, in both agriculture and geology; the other, 'hard' research and long, by trial and error. The latter kind has been, for most of history, more usual. Men have settled in different lands, tried different crops, sought for minerals. Sometimes they have been successful and paved

[1] 'It is a pity, I think, having regard to the comfortable competency secured out of the Colony by successful merchants, that practically none have elected to remain in the country on retirement' ('British Honduras', an address by Sir Eric Swayne in 1917, *Geographical Journal*, vol. L, no. 3).

the way for those of their fellows who imitated them; sometimes they have died in the attempt. Nowadays a highly developed country will adopt research programmes while an under-developed one will experiment by means of human beings with the poverty and suffering this must entail for the many unsuccessful. British Honduras could open itself to immigration in an attempt to try the second method. It does not, because it has already experimented with settlement schemes, which have not been very successful. Sometimes the soil of the settlement was not suitable. Sometimes the capital of the settlers was insufficient. Failure entails a drift to the towns and an increasing burden of population to maintain. In other times, when the social sense of communities was less developed, the unsuccessful could be left to decline and die. Today this is not practicable. In any case, this method of research takes centuries to produce its results.

A compromise between the two must be sought. A proportion of the funds available should be devoted to a certain amount of careful research, and, on the basis of that, a certain amount of settlement and immigration, with adequate capital. The fewer, smaller and more carefully watched the early settlements the better. The later ones would benefit from their errors. As experience was gained, more and more settlements with a snowball effect could be started. It would be hoped that gradually more and more money could be devoted to an actual settlement and development as the settlements were bringing more produce to market and deflating local prices, so that when the local market was saturated and settlements increasing, the local economy would have been sufficiently deflated to make exports a practicable proposition. This, however, is a slow and unspectacular policy, and is unlikely to appeal to those who wish to evoke an emotional response to their policy. (It would be interesting to know if the increase of governmental information services had had any effect in increasing the output of showy and meretricious 'plans'. The production of impressive plans has now become one of the functions of the career civil servant, and at times he seems convinced by his own propaganda in favour of his brain-children. In those cases one has to fall back on the good sense and sanity of the Colonial Office and sometimes those of the Lords Commissioners of His Majesty's Treasury.) The alternative is 'hard' research, measured in individuals' sufferings, although it may masquerade as 'soft' research, that is, much money pouring into it may be an accompanying factor.

PORTHCAWL
December 1949

POSTSCRIPT

It is impossible for economics not to bear an emotional colouring. I had hoped that what I had written was reasonably objective. Soon after writing it I discussed West Indian settlement in British Honduras with a well-known West Indian economist. It was then that I realised that I was biased, and also that he was biased. He considered the problem from the point of view of the West Indian surplus of population. He was not interested in the population of British Honduras. I am. All along I have put the British Honduran first and considered settlement as it affects him. As, however, Honduras needs immigrants as much as the West Indians need to emigrate, there should be little difference in our views. Yet there is.

Probably almost any sort of emigration would improve the lot of the West Indian. I want to see immigrants integrated in the community of Honduras, because it has valuable qualities which are all too rare today. They are a proud and independent community, with that pride and independence which are found in a community where there are few or no rich. Until they had Crown Colony status imposed on them in the last century they ran their own affairs through a Town Meeting, which must have been the nearest approach to true democracy since the days of the Greek city state.[1] Their independence and self-reliance are aided by the poverty of the daily press, so that almost anyone you speak to about local affairs will tell you what he thinks and not merely what he has read in his favourite paper, which is the affliction of the political scene in Europe. What he thinks will be based on his own experience or the

[1] 'We have to remember that the people of British Honduras have always been the freest people on earth. They originally had a public assembly which elected its own magistrates, and those magistrates carried out the laws which the public assembly, that is, the whole people, chose to adopt' ('British Honduras', an address by Sir Eric Swayne in 1917, *Geographical Journal*, vol. L, no. 3).

interchange of experiences with others. To move from Belize straight into the atmosphere of a British general election, as I did, was staggering. There one became accustomed to hearing serious opinions and valuing them, as they were based on facts known to the speaker. In Britain one heard continual argument over matters of which the speaker could not possibly know the facts, and quotations of arguments which one knew already, as one had, like one's companion, read them only that day in the newspapers.[1]

There are solid and valuable qualities in a society where a large part of the population is, in a personal sense, economically independent and where the froth of emotion and disputation based on opinions bought at second hand for a penny a day is absent. There is value too in a society where the individual is adaptable and not too highly specialised. Such a society tends to have a stability and protection from the buffets of fate which rock more highly developed communities, where *mass* production and *mass* unemployment and *total* war are the order of successive days. Such a society, like others, gives way before a drought like that of 1949, perhaps more so, when a state approaching starvation exists for a lot of subsistance farmers. Not all the population can take to the sea and fishing, as so many did during the 1931 crisis.

These are the arguments with which I rationalise my emotional attitude towards British Honduras. The reader can judge how far it vitiates my opinions. If he feels the same, he will like my opinions; if not, he will dislike them. I only hope that if he dislikes them he cannot counter them.

Such a society as I have described cannot be rich in goods, but it can be rich in human quality. There is a temptation to leave it alone. There is probably a sound feeling behind this temptation. Its resilience in the face of adversity probably

[1] I was asked (as an expert on the strength of having passed through Bechuanaland by train six times and a small corner on foot twice) what I thought of the Seretse Khama affair. When I said that I didn't know enough about it to have any particularly valuable thoughts, my interlocutor said in amazement, 'But you *must* have an opinion about it.' This is symptomatic of the purely emotional treatment of affairs in a developed democracy.

leaves it a good deal happier, and it is certainly easier to govern, even if it governs itself. To some extent the question is similar to the problem of migrant labour in Africa. The migrant labourer is inefficient; he spends a couple of years at work, acquiring perhaps some skill; he returns to his village and his 'garden' until the need for cash sends him out again. By this time his skill is forgotten. Government is torn between a desire to maintain what is, in effect, an automatic social security system, as the man who still has ties with his village can always return and be allotted a plot to cultivate, even if his wife has not been cultivating his plot all the time in his absence, and a desire to increase the productivity of the country and to raise the living standards and wages of the worker.[1] British Honduras cannot be left alone. I have tried to show why, and I have tried to show how it can be changed with the least loss of its human and social qualities.

[1] This is not, by any means, the whole problem of migrant labour.

NAIROBI
May 1950

APPENDIX A

NOTE ON THE DEVALUATION OF THE BRITISH HONDURAS DOLLAR

This account was written before the devaluation of the British Honduras dollar on 2 January 1950. It is stated in the Financial Secretary's Report for 1949 that the reasons for devaluation were, in brief:

(*a*) that American demand for mahogany and chicle slumped in 1949 and that the trend of trade had turned away from the dollar area to the sterling area;

(*b*) that 'the producers of pine lumber, grapefruit and fruit juices soon found that their export market in the sterling area was very adversely affected by' the devaluation of sterling while the British Honduras dollar was not devalued; and

(*c*) that there was a lack of confidence in the British Honduras dollar, which was 'exhibited in many different ways'.

The first argument is borne out by the figures in Table II, which shows the hard and soft currency imports, domestic exports and re-exports for the years 1944-9. The story which the figures tell is, however, slightly more complicated than that. Imports from the sterling area increased steadily in those years as communications, especially those with the U.K., became easier after the war. After 1947 a shipping line plied fairly regularly between Liverpool and Belize. At the same time exchange control, in view of the dollar position of the U.K., was being much more strictly applied. There were thus both a return to more normal conditions and official pressure to encourage trade with the sterling area. In 1949, after the devaluation of sterling, there was a period when the cheapness of sterling goods gave a further fillip to this trend and gave hope of some reduction in the cost of living. From 1944 to 1948 dollar imports, while fluctuating with no pattern, remained fairly constant, until the uncertainties of the U.S. market in 1949, coupled with overstocking and the fear of a fall in prices, caused a slump in the demand for mahogany and chicle. As a result, imports and exports from and to the U.S. fell. These are to a large extent complementary.

When the U.S. demand is high there is an increase in imports of machinery and other supplies, including food, for the extraction of mahogany and chicle. Similarly, imports and re-exports increase in both directions. Nevertheless, even in 1949, over two-thirds of imports came from dollar sources.

The effect of devaluation, as far as imports are concerned, is to increase greatly the cost of living and to lower immediately real wages. The larger wage agreements concluded in the Colony in recent years provide for adjustments to meet changes in the cost of living, and there will be pressure from workers not covered by such agreements for increased pay. There is every likelihood of wage rates rising even if they do not reach their old real level. The rise will, no doubt, be partly checked by judiciously subsidising items included in the cost of living index. We have already noted that the development of agriculture is dependent on a reduction in nominal wages. The general effect of devaluation will be the opposite of this. As a long-term policy this has defects.

As a temporary policy to meet the second argument devaluation may have been essential. Both the pine and citrus industries export to the sterling area. The value of the pine industry is that it gives employment to forest workers and thereby supplements the declining mahogany industry. The effect of devaluation of sterling was sharp. 'Nineteen mills were in operation at various times during the year. Some suspended operations for a short period after devaluation of the English pound and at the end of the year there were thirteen in operation; two of which have ceased work indefinitely.' [1]

If, however, imports from dollar sources continue at anything like their reduced 1949 rate and wage rates are increased towards meeting the increased cost of food imports, the net result will only benefit pine exporters if real wages are kept below their pre-devaluation level; that is to say, if any increase in wage rates is insufficient to meet the increased cost of living. The time lag before wage rates start to rise is, however, useful and enables the industry to carry on and some workers to get employment in a slump period. In fact, 'following the devaluation of the English pound in September one exporter of citrus and two of pine lumber reduced the wages of approximately 300 employees by 10 per cent. because of losses which they were experiencing on shipments to sterling areas.' [2] It is not stated, however, what categories of workers these were, nor how

[1] *Annual Report on the Working of the Labour Department for the year ended 31st December 1949.*

[2] *Ibid.*

their rates compared with those in other industries, so that we cannot be sure how significant this was.

The citrus industry is in rather a different category as it operates in a particular area from which it draws its workers. The orchards, unlike most 'farms' in the Colony, are in the hands of a few estate owners. The brunt of devaluation of the British Honduras dollar was therefore passed directly on to the workers in the industry. Table XII shows the progress of the citrus industry in the years 1944-8.

It was only in 1946 that exports were able to restart on any scale, the export of pulp in 1944 being to Jamaica. A comparison of the 1946 figure with the detailed Output Table shows that the net value to the Colony of the grapefruit industry is about 50 per cent. of the value of its exports. To this must be added the various tertiary services, transport, etc., which it brings into being, as, unlike the timber industries, grapefruit does not undertake its own transport. This can be assessed very roughly, at 10 per cent of the value of exports. The industry contributed 10·2 per cent of the value output of agriculture and employed, as owners or employees, about 5 per cent of those engaged in agriculture. It is thus an asset to the Colony, but its importance seems to be generally overestimated.

The lack of confidence in the British Honduras dollar was chiefly exhibited by those persons who had funds in British Honduras and who transferred them to the U.K., in anticipation of the devaluation of the British Honduras dollar, for which they then pressed. This was not so much a lack of confidence as a speculation.

The currency was backed by sterling securities and all government investments were in sterling. The amount required to make good the depreciation of all these investments and the Currency Board Special Account was about $1,500,000. This would presumably have been met by a special grant or an increased grant-in-aid. Whether this sum is greater or less than will be required to meet the expenditure resulting from devaluation, subsidies, relief work and the building of the Stann Creek–Cayo road (this should be one of the greater benefits of devaluation) remains to be seen.

Another factor which probably helped to decide the matter was that capital investment to implement the Evans Commission Report would have to come from sterling sources, and more money would be needed. Taking it by and large, devaluation may be said to have left the employers where they were, benefited the speculators and lowered the real wages of the workers. It should give a further and more powerful wrench to the economy in the direction of the sterling area.

One would, however, have expected some middle rate between the old and new values of the British Honduras dollar (in terms of the U.S. dollar) to have been adopted, as reducing considerably the impact of devaluation on the worker and mitigating the difficulties of the producer for sterling markets, thus sharing more evenly the burden between all classes.

APPENDIX B

DATA NEEDED FOR ANNUAL TABLES

The tables given in this study are built up on the basis of the Census. It is unfortunate that they can only be calculated for one year; and even that year is a slightly generalised year in that some figures were borrowed from other years, where it was thought that they would be near enough to the 1946 figures, if one had had them. Even tables for one year have a value, but they are likely to lose that value in time, and they should be kept up to date. I considered the possibility of extending these tables on an annual basis, but found that, dependent as I was on the data collected by others for different purposes, and not having a statistical office to collect the minimum data which were essential at certain crucial points, I could not produce later tables which would be satisfying to myself and not misleading to others. I believe that tables have been produced by someone for Turkey with projections for ten years into the future! The layman must, at the best of times, be suspicious of national income calculations which put an apparently exact value on certain assumptions which the calculator makes. In a small economy like that of British Honduras, where many people are very familiar with certain parts of the economy, any serious errors in projecting the tables—and I felt that I could not be sure of guarding against them—would seriously increase that suspicion.

Many of the data needed could, however, be fairly readily supplied by the various departments' existing machinery, and most of it would be useful, if it is not necessary to the departments which would collect it. The very generalised statements on agricultural production which appear in the reports of the Department of Agriculture have already been noticed, statements so broad that, even if correct, they have little value, and they might be invalidated if actual figures were collected. On the whole, it should not be necessary for any department to collect data for national income purposes other than those which it should need for the proper carrying out of its own functions.

The Output Table has been the backbone of these calculations, and I will take the data needed to build it up first.

Agriculture. The figures which I used were taken from two censuses of production made in 1943 and 1947. The Agricultural Department has officers stationed in every district and should be able without difficulty to make these censuses every year, in the course of its officers' touring. The censuses, which are based on the acreage planted, should be accompanied by reports on the weather conditions and some value judgments of the return per acre in different regions. The return must vary according to the different soil types and the weather experienced, and more accurate figures should be available than those which I have used, calculating as I did on a return per acre of any crop over the whole Colony. It should be possible to make a cross-check on these figures by comparing them with the figures of crops bought by the Marketing Board in regions where the Board buys the bulk of the surplus. Thus when the acreage returns and the weather conditions suggested increased production one would expect to find a corresponding increase in the Marketing Board's purchases. All these are basic agricultural data which are necessary for the proper working of the Agricultural Department, and their provision in the Department's reports is desirable. If these could be supplemented by further data on the market prices of the various crops, which would also be useful departmental statistics, the Department would be able to draw up its own table of output for agriculture. I doubt whether the Department could produce any valid figures for the numbers engaged in agriculture, as these would vary so much from one part of the year to another.

Quarrying. The Public Works Department should be able to supply from its accounts accurate figures of the numbers engaged in quarrying, their earnings and the value of the output. The item is relatively unimportant and should be readily obtainable by an inquirer on the spot.

Fishing. This presents more of a problem, as it is not under the care of any particular department. The figures which I used were obtained from the Census and cross-checked with the data which the Collector of Customs was collecting for fisheries research, and even then gaps were filled in with some lucky statistical finds. As long as anyone is engaged in fisheries research, he should be able to produce similar figures of fish sold in markets, together with market prices, and, if he had the same knowledge of the coast as Mr R. K. Masson, to extend those figures for the unmarketed fish caught and consumed or exported outside the official export tables. The export of lobsters in 1946, which was recorded only in the United States, is a more difficult matter to deal with, but there is a better Customs control of these exports now which should result in the bulk being included in the official figures. The export by Caribs in the south, which was a residual item in my calculations, resulting from the cross-check of numbers engaged and their estimated earnings, based on the Census, would not be available in that way in a year in which there was no Census. Again, however, anyone familiar with that part of the coast should, in consultation with the District Commissioner in Punta Gorda, be able to make a reasonable estimate. It might be difficult to require anyone engaged in fisheries research to provide the figures and make the estimates required above, although the economics of fishing would presumably be important to him. If it could not be done, it would still be possible for the person constructing the tables to use the market cash-books as a rough basis and, by making inquiries along the coast, arrive at a reasonable estimate.

Forestry. The Forest Department Report already gives a great deal of detail on production, value, etc. The two main items which it lacks are estimates of the value of domestic consumption of timber, which might be a very difficult figure to estimate but which no one could do as well as the Conservator of Forests, and the relation between cuttings, production of sawn timber and exports. The export figures are not related to the production figures and the discrepancy suggests that this is an industry where stocks on hand would have some significance for the national income. With these figures supplied, the preparation of an Account for Timber-getting and Sawmilling on the model given in the text would present no great difficulty and would provide the Forest Department with a useful cross-check on the data which it has collected.

The chicle industry is already well documented as to numbers engaged, production and prices.

Manufacturing and Repair. It is necessary to have data to replace the Census figures in the calculation of this item. These will depend on the figures given in the Labour Department Report, which gives details of employees in a number of industries and of wage rates. The item will always be a difficult one without the Census, as it contains a large number of individual craftsmen, apprentices, etc., in industries for which only an arbitrary classification can be made. The separation of the numbers of employees working in any particular industry is bound to be uncertain, as the industries are not sufficiently clearly defined and employees may easily pass from one to the other without it being noticed. It is possible that the employees in the minor groups, where there are few, could be reclassified differently without the classification being any more right or wrong than it is now. The best that can be done is for the Labour Department to cover a wider and wider range of industries in its report and to make estimates of earnings in the different groups. That is to say, that the actual figures at present given in the Labour Department's Reports should be increased and supplemented with estimates for the rest of the field. Fortunately it is unlikely that any new activity will be started or an old one dropped, in a small community, without the Labour Officer being aware of it. If he makes suitable inquiries directed to finding out the numbers engaged and the earnings in any field during the course of his work in the year, he should be able to produce reasonably accurate estimates. Again, no one can do it so well as he.

For certain industries more detail will be available in the Income Tax Department, and this can be cross-checked with the Labour Department's figures. In some cases the Income Tax figures will be complete for an industry. The national income calculator will have to do the cross-checking and calculations himself, as no one department can produce complete figures. All that can be done is to piece together as full information as is obtainable from the Labour Department, the Income Tax Department and the accounts of government enterprises.

Construction. Building construction presents similar problems to those of manufacturing and repair. It is mainly a craft industry, and many of those engaged in it are self-employed. In the Census only four in the industry were described as employers and 138 were working on their own account. Once again estimates would have to be made, based on information in the Labour Department, the Income Tax Department and the accounts of the Public Works Department.

Road construction is wholly undertaken by the Public Works Department and the obtaining of the figures presents no great difficulty.

The other items in the Output Table would need to be calculated in much the same way, with the help of such additional information as is available in particular groupings, viz. the numbers of public service vehicle licences, draymen's licences, air passenger arrival and departure figures, numbers of registered professional men, and any others. The main difficulty is that the collection of much of this data which is required to replace the ready aid of the Census is time-consuming, and it is unlikely that anyone will have the time in which to do it. To overcome this it would be necessary to parcel out as much of the collection of the data as possible between departments with, as I have tried to show, some advantage to the departments themselves, and the assembling of the data in a form which can easily be used without further inquiry by the calculator. To achieve this the various departments should be required to publish the information in their annual reports; the Agricultural Department a table of output at market prices; the Public Works Department an account for quarrying; the Collector of Customs or the Fisheries Research officer a table of output of fishing at market prices to supplement the export figures in the Customs Report; the Forest Department accounts for timber-getting and sawmilling and for chicle-bleeding; the Labour Department tables of estimated numbers employed and average earnings in the various secondary industries included in the Census. If this were done, then, together with the data already published, the Government accounts and the information in the hands of the Income Tax Department, the final assembly of the figures into national income tables should be fairly simple. It remains to suggest who should do this, a matter I discuss with some trepidation (but less as I am no longer in British Honduras). Three officers seem to be suitably placed for this. The Assessor of Income Tax would be able to bring considerable personal knowledge to bear, through his investigation of accounts and his familiarity with income tax returns. He would, perhaps, be better able, too, to guard against revealing any confidential information through national income figures, which is a particular danger in a small community. If he were not to compile the tables, it might be worth while for him to add to his report a table of profits classified under the various industry groupings. This would not be such a difficult matter for him as for anyone else to do, as he would merely have to apportion each income assessed between its sources in this, that or the other industry. No one else looking at the assessments can make more than the roughest guesses. Over a large number of incomes such guesses probably even out fairly accurately, but in a small community one man's income may be an appreciable factor.

The Financial Secretary, who is also Chief Collector of Income Tax and has access to Income Tax Department files, seems equally suitable, more especially as he would be the one to make use of the tables. Having access to all Government's financial files he also has a great deal of varied information and data which are not available to anyone else, currency movements, bits of statistics acquired haphazardly, and so on, all of which if fitted into the tables would help to make them more accurate. He can ask for and obtain information which no one else can, and if the responsibility for the tables is his, he will realise when useful information is obtainable in the course of his duties. There is, however, an obvious disadvantage in the person who is to use the tables being the same as the one who compiles them. Government policy may, quite unintentionally, govern the form of, and the assumptions in, the tables instead of being governed by them.

The other officer is the Principal Auditor, who also has access to Income Tax files and is, in fact, more familiar with them, through his audit, than the Financial Secretary. He can also utilise them as sources of information and cross-checks on other information. His position, the independence of which from Government is protected, should ensure that the tables do not come under any general suspicion and are freely accepted as a fair basis for economic policy. He has the advantage of a wider actual knowledge of the Colony than the others, as his tours take him to all parts every year, where he can acquire many data, on the spot, and he has an intimate knowledge of the workings and activities of all departments. He is in a better position to see the economy as a whole. The information he learns in conversation is likely to be more accurate as people are not concerned, as he has no part in Government policy and is not a sufficiently 'important' figure, to tell him what they think he wants to hear, or to tell him things which they hope will influence his decisions in one way or another.

TABLE I

POPULATION AND MAJOR SETTLEMENTS CENSUS OF BRITISH HONDURAS, 9 APRIL 1946

Total	59,220		
Belize District		26,781	
Belize Town			21,884
Belize River to Big Falls			1,988
Northern River			1,032
Ambergris Cay and Cay Caulker			666
Manatee River			510
Sibun River			449
Northern District		12,293	
Corozal Town			2,190
Orange Walk Town			1,395
San Estevan			282
Cayo District		7,370	
Cayo Town			1,548
Benque Viejo			1,264
Stann Creek District		6,373	
Stann Creek Town			3,414
Stann Creek Valley			649
Sittee River and All Pines			538
Commerce Bight			510
Seine Bight			505
Toledo District		6,403	
Punta Gorda			1,375
San Antonio			1,099
Toledo Settlement			771

TABLE II

IMPORTS, EXPORTS AND RE-EXPORTS

	Imports		*Domestic Exports*		*Re-Exports*	
	A	B	A	B	A	B
Value in $000—						
1944	435	6929	222	1638	14	4213
1945	406	7431	110	1866	11	2935
1946	893	5890	851	2662	32	1677
1947	1103	7553	1067	3176	25	1874
1948	1582	6493	1882	2659	37	1574
1949 [1]	2194	3796	2499	873	51	1141

A = Empire, excluding Canada.

B = Other countries plus Canada. The proportion relating to soft currency countries is very small.

Taken from Customs Reports, 1944-9.

[1] Transhipment cargoes excluded from 1949 figures.

Percentages—						
1944	5·9	94·1	11·9	88·1	0·3	99·7
1945	5·2	94·8	5·5	94·5	0·4	99·6
1946	13·2	86·8	24·2	75·8	1·5	98·5
1947	12·8	87·2	25·1	74·9	1·3	98·7
1948	19·6	80·4	41·5	58·5	2·3	97·7
1949	31·1	68·9	74·1	25·9	4·3	95·7

TABLE III

PERCENTAGE PRINCIPAL DOMESTIC EXPORTS, 1944-9

	Mahogany Logs	Mahogany Lumber	Bananas	Chicle	Coconuts	Grapefruit	Grapefruit Juices	Pine Lumber
1944	12·72	30·23	4·64	36·44	7·44	0·13	—	0·48
1945	17·35	27·28	3·07	29·86	13·73	0·07	—	0·91
1946	10·00	34·18	1·39	28·86	5·68	0·02	9·06	4·83
1947	16·76	25·68	2·03	30·90	3·55	0·01	9·82	3·70
1948	21·53	24·87	1·43	19·63	3·40	0·01	9·45	9·22
1949	3·82	34·06	1·72	15·11	2·44	6·84	8·56	17·62

TABLE IV

PERCENTAGE DISTRIBUTION OF TRADE, 1944-9

	U.K.	Canada	Jamaica	Other Empire	U.S.A.	Mexico	Guatemala	Other
IMPORTS								
1944	3·34	5·96	2·20	0·37	40·53	29·54	11·82	6·24
1945	4·23	12·83	0·52	0·43	47·60	21·44	9·23	3·72
1946	9·07	21·15	1·86	2·24	51·71	7·28	3·12	3·57
1947	9·61	14·21	0·75	2·38	56·00	8·79	3·70	4·56
1948	15·42	14·65	1·42	2·75	43·23	11·03	5·05	6·45
1949[1]	30·10	11·97	1·06	5·47	38·83	0·92	0·01	11·64
DOMESTIC EXPORTS								
1944	—	12·79	11·93	0·03	74·48	0·61	—	0·16
1945	0·03	8·97	5·54	0·01	84·44	0·72	—	0·29
1946	16·37	28·59	7·85	0·01	45·65	0·56	0·13	0·84
1947	20·96	15·79	4·33	0·57	55·01	0·45	0·27	2·62
1948	28·85	18·92	12·37	0·22	37·62	0·19	0·21	1·62
1949	50·27	2·26	20·28	3·56	20·91	0·20	0·02	2·50

[1] 1949 excludes transhipment cargoes.

TABLE V

COST OF LIVING INDEX, 1942-9

1939 = 100

Item and weight—	*Food 71*	*Rent 12*	*Clothing 14*	*Fuel, Light and Washing 10*	*Other 10*	*Total*
31st December 1942	156	100	200	141	125	151
1943	159	100	206	132	135	154
1944	168	100	201	140	138	160
1945	168	100	214	142	144	162
1946	200	110	307	165	160	197
1947	219	110	287	167	160	206
1948	214	110	325	188	172	211
1949 [1]	192	110	295	172	173	193

[1] This shows the effect of the devaluation of sterling before the devaluation of the British Honduras dollar, and a temporary fall in American food prices.

Taken from Annual Reports of the Labour Department.

TABLE VI

RELATION OF IMPORTS AND EXPORTS OF PINE AND HARDWOODS FOR THE YEARS 1944-9 BY VALUE IN $000

	Imports		*Domestic Exports*		*Re-exports*	
	Hard	*Pine*	*Hard*	*Pine*	*Hard*	*Pine*
1944	2338	14	808	18	2961	—
1945	1884	3	939	19	1936	1
1946	42	7	1625	170	338	2
1947	548	11	1994	157	811	—
1948	593	83	2315	443	461	1
1949 [1]	—	11	1391	594	166	—

[1] Transhipment cargoes excluded in 1949. (From Customs Reports.)

PERCENTAGE OF HARD AND PINE WOODS TO TOTAL DOMESTIC TIMBER EXPORTS

1944	97·82	2·18
1945	98·02	1·98
1946	90·53	9·47
1947	92·70	7·30
1948	83·94	16·06
1949	70·06	29·94

TABLE VII

IMPORTS, DOMESTIC EXPORTS AND RE-EXPORTS OF CHICLE FOR THE YEARS 1940-9 BY VALUE IN $000

(From Customs Reports)

	Imports	*Domestic Exports*	*Re-exports*
1940	430	397	534
1941	486	620	533
1942	235	356	326
1943	—	505	—
1944	456	678	418
1945	254	590	354
1946	353	1014	390
1947	359	1311	359
1948	237	891	553
1949 [1]	—	510	—

[1] Transhipment cargoes excluded in 1949. This table shows that the proportion of workers over the border is by no means constant. It also shows that in nearly every year, as with timber, the re-exports considerably exceed the imports. This is interesting from an administrative point of view. but only suggests that there are large unrecorded imports.

TABLE VIII

IMPORTS, PRODUCTION AND EXPORTS OF SUGAR FOR THE YEARS 1944-9 IN TONS

	Imports	*Production*	*Exports*
1944	220	1024	—
1945	885	456	—
1946	1060	809	—
1947	300	1178	—
1948	651	1043	—
1949	149	2108	352

Imports, except in 1947 and 1948 when 122 tons and 474 tons of unrefined sugar were imported to supplement local factory production, were of refined sugar. The share of sugar production in the national income is usually greater than the share shown for 1946. The large imports in 1945 and 1946 were due to purchases on Government account, owing to a breakdown of the factory's machinery in 1945.

TABLE IX

PRODUCTION OF RUM FOR THE YEARS 1944-9 IN LIQUID GALLONS

1944	30,486
1945	20,820
1946	16,928
1947	29,208
1948	26,534
1949	35,486

The share of rum production in the national income is, therefore, usually greater than the share shown for 1946.

TABLE X

PRODUCTION OF CIGARETTES IN 1000S

1944	22,498
1945	23,008
1946	23,792
1947	22,998
1948	28,625
1949	30,171

The increase from 1947 to 1949 reflects the more stringent application of exchange control and the cessation of imports of American cigarettes. (Such as were obtainable from smugglers thereby became cheaper, being duty-free.)

TABLE XI

MOVEMENTS OF AIRCRAFT PASSENGERS, 1942-9

	Arrivals	*Departures*
1942	175	134
1943	288	260
1944[1]	2187	2293
1945	3991	3331
1946	6713	5139
1947	4477	2758
1948	1483	1471
1949	1902	1792

[1] Opening of new airport.

TABLE XII

EXPORTS OF CITRUS, 1944-8, BY VALUE IN $s

	Grapefruit	*Grapefruit Pulp*	*Grapefruit Juice*	*Oranges*	*Orange Juice*
1944	2,432	89,064	—	3,666	—
1945	1,371	—	—	4,900	—
1946	826	—	339,812	3,923	—
1947	527	—	416,904	3,442	—
1948	718	—	429,473	2,511	2,609

TABLE XIII

REVENUE AND EXPENDITURE, 1941-9, IN $000

	True Revenue	*Grant*	*C.D. and W.*	*Other*	*True Expenditure*	*C.D. and W.*[1]	*Other*
1941 . . .	1,230	101	46	200 [4]	1,309	—	214 [4]
1942 . . .	1,269	181	14	186 [4]	1,497	—	139 [4]
1943 . . .	1,428	266	184	—	1,839	—	—
1944 . . .	1,675	173	662	—	2,464	—	—
1945 . . .	1,924	169	412	—	2,530	—	—
1946 . . .	2,206	81	351	—	2,552	—	—
1947 . . .	2,506	—	435	—	2,477	433	—
1948 . . .	2,580	101 [2]	528	—	2,866	529	—
1949 . . .	2,387	340 [3]	555	429 [5]	2,771	647	429 [5]

[1] C.D. and W. Expenditure was shown separately only from 1947. Prior to this it was included in True Expenditure. The C.D. and W. receipts should be added to Revenue for 1941-6.

[2] The grant-in-aid in 1948 was to meet salary increases and arrear payments from 1946 and was not to count for political purposes as a grant-in-aid. The point of this was that if the Colony ceased to be grant-aided for three years it would cease to come under the control of H.M. Treasury.

[3] In 1949 the great drought made relief work necessary.

[4] In 1941 and 1942 grants of $180,000 and $181,978 were given for Relief Schemes. Grants of $19,502 and $52 were made for the Conversion of the Stann Creek Railway to a road.

[5] In 1949 a grant of $428,743 was made to enable the Colony to repay the 1931 Hurricane Loan.

BIBLIOGRAPHY

ANDERSON, A. H. (ed.). *Brief Sketch of British Honduras.* Belize, Government Printer, 1944.

Annual Reports of Agricultural, Audit, Customs, Education, Forestry, Labour, Medical, Survey Departments and Annual Financial Statements of the Colony. Belize, Government Printer.

BURDON, Sir JOHN A. *Archives of British Honduras.* Three volumes. London: vol. I, 1931; vol. II, 1934; vol. III, 1935.

COOK, Lt. *Remarks on a Passage from the River Belize in the Bay of Honduras to Merida, The Capital of the Province of Yucatan in the Spanish West Indies.* (London, 1769.) Facsimile reprint, 1935. University of Louisiana, New Orleans, U.S.A.

DODDS, G. W. *Report on Belize Harbour and some of the Rivers of British Honduras.* Belize, Government Printer, 1936.

DUNLOP, W. R. *Report on the Economic and Natural Features of British Honduras in Relation to Agriculture, with Proposals for Development.* Crown Agents for the Colonies, 1921.

GANN, T. *Mystery Cities.* London, 1925.

GANN, T. *Ancient Cities and Modern Tribes.* London, 1926.

GIBBS, A. R. *British Honduras. An Historical and Descriptive Account of the Colony from its Settlement, 1670.* London, 1883.

HUMMEL, C. *Reports on the Forests of British Honduras, with Suggestions for a Far-reaching Forest Policy.* London, Crown Agents for the Colonies, 1921.

JOYCE, T. A. *Report on the Investigations at Lubaantum, British Honduras, 1926.* London, Royal Anthropological Institute, 1926.

METZGEN, M. S., and CAIN, H. E. C. *The Handbook of British Honduras.* London, The West India Committee, 1925.

Minutes of the Legislative Council. Belize, Government Printer.

MORRIS, W. A. *The Colony of British Honduras, its Resources and Prospects.* London, 1883.

OWER, L. H. *Geology of British Honduras.* Belize, Government Printer, 1928.

Report of the Committee of Nutrition on the Colony of British Honduras. Belize, Government Printer.

Report of the Development and Planning Committee. Belize, Government Printer, 1946.

Report on the Social and Economic Progress of the People of British Honduras. Belize, Government Printer.

STONE, DORIS ZEMURRAY. *Some Spanish Entradas.* New Orleans (Reprint from Middle American Research Series, Publication No. 4 *Middle American Papers*), Department of Middle American Research, University of Louisiana, 1932.

SWAYNE, Sir ERIC. 'British Honduras'. *Geographical Journal*, vol. L, 1917.

THOMPSON, J. E. *Archaeological Investigations in the Southern Cayo District, British Honduras.* Publication No. 301, 1931, Field Museum of Natural History, Chicago.

THOMPSON, J. E. *Excavations at San Jose, British Honduras.* Publication No. 506, 1939, Washington, Carnegie Institution (includes an Index of Maya Sites in British Honduras).

West India Royal Commission Report. London, H.M.S.O.

References, where appropriate, to a few of the many publications dealing with National Income Calculations will be found in the text.

INDEX

INDEX

www.ingramcontent.com/pod-product-compliance
Lightning Source LLC
LaVergne TN
LVHW011520200926
848484LV00001B/87